Understanding Prophetic EVENTS - *2000* - PLUS!

The
ANTICHRIST,
RAPTURE
and the

Battle of
ARMAGEDDON

END TIMES - *SERIES FOUR*

DR. ALAN PATEMAN
Foreword by Dr. Ron Charles

By Dr. Alan Pateman

By Dr. Jennifer Pateman

Available from APMI Publications, Amazon.com and Other Retail Outlets

The ANTICHRIST, RAPTURE and the Battle of ARMAGEDDON

DR. ALAN PATEMAN

BOOK TITLE:
The Antichrist, Rapture and the Battle of Armageddon,
Understanding Prophetic EVENTS-2000-PLUS!

WRITTEN BY Dr. ALAN PATEMAN
ISBN: 978-1-909132-75-7
eBook ISBN: 978-1-909132-76-4

Written in 1996, Released in (Copyright) 2018 Alan Pateman

Published By:
APMI Publications
In Partnership with Truth for the Journey Books **28**
Email: publications@alanpateman.com
www.AlanPatemanMinistries.com

Acknowledgements:
Acknowledgements:
Editing / Proofreading / Research: Dr. Jennifer Pateman
Layout & eBook Marketing: Dorothea Struhlik
Cover Design: Dr.P.
Cover Image Credit: © germanjames, www.fotosearch.com

Dedication

I lovingly dedicate this book to the Jewish people. In opening our eyes to the truth about the Jews and the Jewish people in regard to the Christian World, the Nations and the End Times, we will attempt through these pages to discover that truth and final out come for their destiny and ours. I pray that the Holy Spirit will give you insight into this very often misunderstood reality.

Table of Contents

Foreword

*Eschatology — the study of
the current knowledge of the End-Times**

In our modern society, the word invokes mental images of The Mark of the Beast, Tribulation, Armageddon and the last war to end all wars, and Final Judgment.

Although it has only been in the past 100 years that the word, *eschatology*, has been used as a noun to identify events that deal with the end-times or the time that immediately precedes the end of all things as we know it, teachings

*Note: This Foreword by Dr. Ron Charles is included in all four parts of this End Times Series *(Series One: Israel, the Question of Ownership; Series Two: Earnestly Contending for the State of Israel; Series Three: The Temple, Antichrist and the New World Order; Series Four: The Antichrist, Rapture and the Battle of Armageddon).*

associated with the event, theories proposed to predict the event and philosophies, *(both religious and non-religious),* developed that attempts to explain or clarify the event dating back thousands of years.

The ancient Egyptians taught that the end of the world or the end of all ages, as they called it, would first be preceded by a great apostasy against their historical gods and then a massive return to the worship of the gods just before the end came.

The Assyrians believed that the end will be preceded by a great war on the plains of the Euphrates River between the armies of the West and the armies of the East and that at the height of the war, the sun god would appear bringing eternal peace and punishment to evil ones.

The Babylonians believed that the end will be preceded by a great leader who would cause all people to worship him, as the reincarnated Marduk. Then, when he had firmly established himself as Marduk, that Marduk himself will come and judge and destroy with intense fire, all those who were deceived by the great leader.

In fact, we now know that in virtually all developed societies for the past 5,000 years, from Egypt to Rome and from Assyria to Persia, there has been a belief by those societies that there will indeed be an end to all things and that this will be accompanied by wars and natural tragedies, judgement of all people, rewards for the believing benevolent and righteous, and punishments for the evil and or non-believers.

As it has been for thousands of years, so it is in our society today, with but one major exception—the Jews. It was in the early-19th century in England that a handful of theologians and bible teachers began to dissect the scriptures and discovered what they felt to be a uniform thread of God's compassion and benevolent consistency in dealing with the descendants of Abraham, that stretched throughout the bible from Genesis to Revelation; maintaining its constancy through wars, exile, natural disasters, genocide, and societal extermination.

This belief began to crystallize into a theological position that spread throughout Europe, into America and throughout the world, until by the mid-19th century it had become the accepted doctrine more than the exception in European and American evangelical and fundamental religious circles.

As this doctrine became more accepted in the late 19th century, eschatology specialists began to see how God's dealing with the children of Abraham over the past centuries and the horrors that they were forced to endure, has in fact set the stage for the modern development of the state of national Israel, which in turn is recognized as God's physical end-times epitome whereby these approaching events can more readily be recognized and chronicled.

Dr. Alan Pateman's four part End Times Series *(Series One: Israel, the Question of Ownership; Series Two: Earnestly Contending for the State of Israel; Series Three: The Temple, Antichrist and the New World Order; Series Four: The Antichrist, Rapture and the Battle of Armageddon)*, not only seeks to bring the reader *"up to date"* with regard to present day societal eschatological convictions, showing how Israel is in fact, God's chosen instrument that will be used to chart and to instigate fulfilment of these long anticipated end-time events.

He also accurately traces the history of how the Jews through history have been used as God's instrument; how evil forces have for centuries, all the way up to this present time, sought to destroy these people, their mission, their purpose, and their unique position within the overall plan of God; and how the worldwide entrenchment of modern day apostasy, materialism and deception will immediately proceed the realization of these end-times events, anticipated for so many thousands of years.

Such a work has long been needed that successfully marries the past, especially that of the Jews and of the rise of anti-Semitism, with the events of the future, and clarifies the mysteries of eschatology so that those of us who await the glorious return of our Lord Jesus, can more easily understand and appreciate the inimitability of the exceptional days and times in which we live—the End Times.

Dr. Ron Charles
The Cubit Foundation
www.cubitfoundation.org

Preface

In the year of 1996 my wife and I and our small son lived in the Tuscany area of Italy for the period of nine months. *(This is the duration of time before we moved to Italy in the year 1999).* And up to this time I had been preaching frequently throughout Europe, Africa and America etc., with a measure of success.

One would say that these early years of ministry were powerful and brought me in touch with many wonderful men and women throughout the nations. But one of the most difficult and evading revelations was the whole subject on

*Note: This Preface is included in all four parts of this End Times Series *(Series One: Israel, the Question of Ownership; Series Two: Earnestly Contending for the State of Israel; Series Three: The Temple, Antichrist and the New World Order; Series Four: The Antichrist, Rapture and the Battle of Armageddon).*

the End Times. I'd been to bible school and been successful in ministry yet I did not really have an understanding or should I say *any* understanding about the Jews, the Babylonian structure, the rapture etc.

Then one evening as it became seemingly my custom to read to my family and anyone else who *(team members etc.)* was there in the evenings. I would read from a particular book that God had inspired me to pick up or to take from my shelf. And it was then on one of those quiet, yet warm summer evenings in '96 that I began reading the biography written by Derek Prince, the husband of *(then his first wife)* Lydia Prince. The book was titled *"Appointment in Jerusalem."*

Oh, What a Wonderful Book that Is

I've cried as I've read the pages - as the Holy Spirit touched my own heart - my journey in ministry seemingly has similarities to this story - being led by the Holy Spirit along a life journey to fulfil the call of God. Her journey was to Jerusalem. My journey is to the nations. But wherever God is leading us, He always leads us by his Holy Spirit and we can learn through similarities, not only through the scriptures but also through the testimonies of others and of course the biographies that have been put into writing.

Let me make a statement here, the Holy Spirit is our teacher and He knows what we need to learn or teach us at any given time. Therefore I only read the books or listen to the tapes that He has led me to listen to or read that particular day. He knows what needs to be built into my soul and spirit man - He knows what I need to be fed upon to nourish my very being, He always knows what's up ahead as He's the one that's leading us.

But coming to a place of reading the whole of this special book, *"Appointment in Jerusalem"* God began to speak to me about the End Times. As I picked up a pen and began to make a few notes, I felt the Holy Spirit tell me to get up at 6 o'clock the next morning and begin a time of study because He wanted to reveal to me His plan for the End Times.

Six Weeks in God's Study

Every morning for the next six weeks I got up and the only place that was very quiet where I would not be disturbed was in a garage in the basement of our apartment block. Every morning I would be down there at 6 o'clock praying, studying and writing. Day after day, sometimes for hours at a time or until I felt a release and I knew that the day had finished and a new day would begin tomorrow.

Only there was a woman in the garage next door who had a big knitting machine, which she used to sit at most of the time. At first it used to disturb me with the noise of the thrashing back and forth of her machine! We never met, I never saw what she accomplished in her knitting over those weeks and she would not have had a clue that God Almighty was visiting one of His sons to reveal revelation on a very important subject that most Christians know nothing about.

Six weeks went past and what you have in this four part series on the End Times, *(Series One: Israel, the Question of Ownership; Series Two: Earnestly Contending for the State of Israel; Series Three: The Temple, Antichrist and the New World*

Order; Series Four: The Antichrist, Rapture and the Battle of Armageddon - also incorporated as five course syllabuses within the teaching curriculum of the LICU University) is a result of that time.

I can honestly say that this insight, understanding, revelation and impartation has changed my life. I have such a heart for the Jewish people, for Jerusalem as a Capital of Israel and for what God has in store for this time.

Of course you need to read and ask God to reveal to you by His Spirit, His truth. And together I pray with the same desire as Lydia Prince and ask you and every Christian to pray for Jerusalem.

> Lydia wrote *"I suddenly came to see that we Christians have a debt that has gone unpaid for many centuries – to Israel and to Jerusalem. It is to them that we owe the bible, the prophets, the apostles, the Saviour Himself. For far too long we have forgotten this debt, but now the time has come for us to begin repaying it – and there are two ways that we can do this.*
>
> *First, we need to repent of our sins against Israel: at best, our lack of gratitude and concern, at worst, our open contempt and persecution.*
>
> *Then, out of true love and concern, we must pray as the psalmist tells us, 'for the peace of Jerusalem,' remembering that peace can only come to Jerusalem as Israel turns back to God. God has shown me that from now on to pray in this way for Jerusalem will be the highest form of service that I can render Him."*[1]

CHAPTER 1

Israel, the Church and the Endtimes

Greatest Strategic Deception

In the October issue of the *"McAlvany Intelligence Advisor"* *(1991)*, General Sir Walter Walker, the former NATO commander-in-chief, warned, "We are now in a period of the greatest strategic deception.

Perhaps in all history so I feel I should not allow this occasion to pass without warning you of the future that lies ahead in the next decade. I say most emphatically that the *Cold War is not yet over*, but only in a state of remission...

The Soviet Union is still devoting a vast proportion of its resources to sustain a military machine capable of threatening the west... The Soviet's military threat has not evaporated.

The neutralisation of NATO has long been one of the Soviets prime glasnost deception goals.

I leave you with the stark fact that unless we stand fast and stop the rot, the demonstrable truth is that, contrary to the Kremlin's self-serving pose of humility, the Soviet Union is not *'on the verge of collapse,'* Western defence, on the other hand, is."[1]

It's amazing to think that although Russia is begging the West for vast amounts of food aid and billions in financial assistance they continue to produce six new highly advanced nuclear ballistic submarines every year, costing over three billion dollars each.

When Gorbachev, in 1985 became the leader of the USSR, the Soviet's Red Army was more than four times larger than the U.S military forces. And has a huge lead on America in every single area where weapons and military manpower is concerned.

Consider these weapons production figures:

1985 - 1991 Weapon Production

Weapon:	Russia:	America:	Ratio:
I.C.B.Ms.	715	68	10 to 1
Tanks	16,300	4,891	3 to 1
Armoured Vehicles	28,800	5,375	5 to 1
Bombers	450	104	4 to 1
Submarines	54	24	2 to 1
Sub-launched Missiles	490	205	2 to 1

Source: U.S Defence Intelligence Agency *(taken from Prince of Darkness by Grant R. Jeffrey, p172)*[2]

Grant R. Jeffrey says, "Russian state prosecutor's office released reports of its investigation into the massive disappearance of Soviet gold reserves and billions in western hard currency from the Soviet Union's State Bank. The investigators discovered Gorbachev and his associates established 7200 secret bank accounts in foreign countries, including Switzerland and Panama.

The communist party for the illegal private benefit of their top officials set up the illegal accounts. Over $174 billion in hard currency was given to the USSR for food aid. However, it was diverted and has now disappeared into these illegal foreign accounts. Who authorised these illegal undertakings? Time Magazine's Man of the Year — Mikhail Gorbachev."[3]

President Yeltsin in his attempt to rule the country in its difficult crisis was given sweeping powers over Parliament. These *"dictatorial"* constitution powers could prove to be a time bomb waiting to explode, especially in light of future events.

The Bear and Vodka

Is the *"Man"* with so much pressure concerning global, historical and spiritual, prophetic timing, strong enough to cope?

Turmoil turns the bear into vodka chaser, are the Headline's on *page 45* of the Sunday Express, *(July 7th, 1996)* by Oliver James. He says, *"Yeltsin is under the Couch,"* because Boris Yeltsin failed to arrive at his election photo call last week, the reason given, he had *"a cold."*

Oliver James profiles the Russian president by writing, "Boris Yeltsin has proved many times during his life that he would rather die — literally — than be made passive by misfortune."[4]

While still at university he suffered his first heart attack because he insisted on going to fitness training despite a serious bout of flu. Even though his doctors told him he would probably die, he continued training immediately after the attack.

He wrote, *"The risk of course was colossal however, I reckoned I shouldn't feel sorry for my heart, but rather give it a full workout..."*

Leadership Qualities Forged

The co-author of his autobiography, *Valentin Yumashev,* says: **"His daily schedule would make a normal man collapse."** Yeltsin forces himself to get by with little sleep, saying: *"I schooled myself to do with no more than three or four hours sleep a night from a young age."* People with this level of activity are usually terrified of their own feelings and of being power-less in the face of adversity...

His first acquaintance with vodka came a few days after his birth. The priest who baptised him was so drunk that he dropped the infant into the tub of holy water. *"Yeltsin took his cue from the priest and has famously been falling down drunk in public on many occasions since. But he is probably not an alcoholic — just a man who, from time to time, goes on a binge..."*

Studies of the childhoods of great leaders, especially dictators, almost always reveal severe adversity. And when forced to take a father's place, leadership qualities can be forged. Yeltsin recalls, **"From the age of six the household was in my charge."** With both parents at work, he had to look after his younger siblings, clean and cook.

But adversity alone does not create top leaders. Such men nearly always also have a determined, intelligent and resourceful mother.

It is now 1996 *(at the time of writing)*, time for elections, what will happen to Yeltsin's continued reform program? Who will come to power? This is vital when we think of *"End Times."* If Zhirinovsky wins, the world will face an incredibly dangerous and nuclear-armed *"Hitler."*

No Democracy without Violence

Vladimir Zhirinovsky is an *"imperialist"* and the leader of the Liberal Democrat Party. Grant Jeffrey says, "This man appeared out of nowhere to win six million votes in the 1991 Presidential Election, coming in third behind Yeltsin. After the election he declared, *'When I come to power, I will be a dictator. Russia needs a dictator.'*

Zhirinovsky's slogan **'No democracy without violence'** warns us of terrible days ahead for Russia. In the parliamentary elections of December 1993, to the surprise of everyone, Zhirinovsky won the highest number of seats in the Russian Duma and the balance of power...

In only two years, Zhirinovsky may become the president of a resurgent Russian Empire intent on conquering its neighbours. He stunned audiences on a German radio program threatening them with nuclear destruction if Germany interfered in Russian affairs. Later he warned Japan, *'We will create new Hiroshimas and Nagasakis. I will not hesitate to use nuclear weapons.'* His program calls for re-militarising Russia and a massive increase in foreign arms sales. Who is he? Who is secretly supporting his plan to rule Russia?

Despite his strange comments many Russians find his tough and belligerent approach attractive. His irresponsible statement — *'Vote for me and I will give you everything you want'* — appeals to many disillusioned voters. In addition he promises to restore Russian pride and power...

His Liberal Democratic Party is neither liberal nor democratic. It is an extremely nationalistic, fascist, imperialistic and Neo-Nazi party. Zhirinovsky proposes to conquer Central Asia, the Middle East, and the Persian Gulf. He has threatened Japan, Germany and Lithuania with nuclear devastation. Astonishingly he warns about a new Russian machine gun *'that will establish order in any place.'*

Recently he promised to expand the Russian Empire toward the Indian Ocean and Mediterranean. In addition he promises to execute leaders of organised crime on the spot. He is a skilled political orator promising the voters whatever they want to hear...

Conquering Territories

His 142 page autobiographical book *'The Last March to the South,'* released December 26th, 1993, lays out

Zhirinovsky's plans to conquer the former Soviet Republics, Turkey, Iran, India, Finland, Eastern Europe, the Baltic Republics and the Middle East.

It pictures Russia as a kind of white knight saving *'the south'* while conquering the territories from the Middle East to the Indian Ocean. ***'From Constantinople to Kabul... to the shores of the India Ocean everyone will speak Russian.'***

He wants to recreate the Czarist Russian Empire occupying Poland, Finland and incredibly, Alaska. *'The Dallas Morning News'* on December 14th, 1993, reported that he warned of future conflicts with Iraq, Azerbaijan, Armenia and Pakistan that 'will make a hell out of these regions, with wars raging for 10-15 years... Cities and roads will be destroyed, epidemics will explode, millions will die and neither America nor the United Nations will be able to do anything about it.

The world community will beg Russia to save what remains of those peoples in Central Asia, the Middle East and the Indian Ocean. We will be obliged to send our boys there. Our army will then appear on the coast of the India Ocean.'"[5]

Even if Zhirinovsky never wins a presidential election, the fact is that the people of Russia have on the most part shown that they want a "DICTATOR." One thing is for sure, as Deputy Prime Minister Chubais has warned that Zhirinovsky's policies would lead to disaster.

"If we try to fulfil his policies," *he said,* ***"there will be World War Three."***

CHAPTER 2

Putin - Who is He?

Update 2000

David Hathaway and his co-writer say that, Yeltsin, master of Russian drama, took his final curtain on the eve of the New Millennium. Instead of the expected New Year's political speech, Yeltsin announced, *"I am addressing you for the last time as President… I want to ask your forgiveness, because many of our hopes have not come true, because what we thought would be easy has turned out to be painfully difficult. I ask you to forgive me."*

Yeltsin championed the demise of communism in 1991, but saw Russia become a land, not of hope, but of violence, corrupt riches and extreme poverty, sickness, tuberculosis, spiralling alcoholism, drug addiction, prostitution, homelessness, abandoned children.

Putin, plucked out of obscurity on 9th August 1999 to be Yeltsin's fifth Prime Minister in only 2 years, Putin seemed destined to be just another *"Yeltsin victim in the making."* Last September his popularity rating was only 2%. Now he is President! But who is he?

In his first address to the nation as acting president in January, he promised to uphold "freedom of speech, freedom of conscience, freedom of religion, freedom of the press, the right to private property etc..." But he had a classic KGB career, never resigned from the communist part, and in 1998, Yeltsin made him head of the FSB *(successor to the KGB)*.

So, is he at heart a democrat, a trustworthy custodian of Russia's new *"civil liberties"* – or is he committed to the old KGB ways? His ascent to power has coincided with mounting pressure and intimidation on the Russian press. It is also reported that, since January, Stalin is being openly rehabilitated as a political role model; Putin is acting out Yeltsin's secret alliance with the communist party, and has begun the process of re-militarising the nation.

What will happen now?

The Russian people have elected a question mark:

Putin has promised to restore law and order to a chaotic, crime-ridden country, but how? His theory is: *"You have to hit first and hard, so that your opponent will not get to his feet."* He applied this to the destruction of Chechnya, Russia's version of NATO's intervention in Kosovo.

Serving as a vent for pent-up public frustration after years of economic decline, diminishing influence abroad and international humiliation by the US, Putin's action is immensely popular with the Russian people.

Putin's Nuclear Option

The first decree signed by acting President Vladimir Putin in January was a new National Security Doctrine lowering the threshold for the use of nuclear weapons. It allows Russia to use her vast nuclear arsenal to *"repel armed aggression."*

At the same time, with 75% of Russia's current conventional weaponry obsolete, Putin increased military investment by 50%. Russia is currently developing a new generation of low-yield nuclear weapons for *"precision"* non-strategic strikes, 10 years in advance of anything in the West. Where does the money come from? **The IMF?**

But Russia is a bear in need of a wolf to fight. The more Russia declines politically and economically, the more she feels marginalised in world affairs and under pressure from US and NATO in Europe and the Middle East, the more dangerous she becomes.

Intelligence Digest writes: *"A weakened Russia, fearful of foreign intervention in its internal affairs but incapable of deterring it with conventional military power, is clearly indicating that it is willing to rattle nuclear sabres to cool the ardour of anyone seen to be threatening Russia."*

Russia's alliance with China and Iran

Under Yeltsin and now under Putin, former rivals Russia and China are working on an anti-NATO alliance, fearing that the Western nations *"are trying to build a world order convenient only for them."*

Intelligence Digest writes that "any further major moves by the US to forge a New World Order in its image *(such as another Kosovo-style military intervention)* will only strengthen the opposition of the growing anti-Western bloc led by Russia and China." Russia's new military doctrine *(14 January 2000),* confirms China as her *"strategic ally"* determined to resist US global dominance.

Russia is extending her military influence in the Middle East, regardless of her own economic and political crisis. In Moscow on 13 January Russia and Iran affirmed their support for a *"multipolar"* world, to resist US global control. Putin's Russia does not intend to be pushed about by the US.

All this is in response to the perceived threat posed in April 1999 when, to celebrate its 50th anniversary, NATO published a new strategic concept, declaring it is prepared **"to safeguard the freedom and security of its members by political and military means."**

Does NATO mean it will not shrink from the use of force when it suits? As in Kosovo *(1999)?* Seen as a forceful new thrust towards US internationalism, it backfired, triggering a powerful transglobal anti-Western alliance including Russia, China and Arab countries.

Intelligence Digest Reports

"NATO…appears to believe it can do more or less what it likes, when it likes, where it likes… Russia's weakness will increase the dangers… Lacking the wherewithal to resist the United States with conventional forces, Russia is set to become ever more reliant upon tactical, battle-fighting, nuclear weapons."

As a result of NATO's bombing campaign in Yugoslavia and its perceived aggressive expansion into former Russian satellite territories, Russia froze its ties with the West. NATO then clashed with Russia over its brutal campaign in Chechnya.

However, at a meeting with Russia's Defence minister in February, NATO's Secretary General praised Russia as a world power and reaffirmed Russia and NATO's shared responsibility to patrol peace in such areas as Kosovo. He said, *"I think we have moved from the permafrost into slightly softer ground."* Have we?

Scripture Predicted

All of this is predicted in scripture as the build up to Antichrist and Armageddon. After communism collapsed in 1991, most concluded that, because Russia's economy and military power drastically declined, it would be impossible to fulfil the prophecies of Ezekiel in our lifetime. Not only is this incorrect, but Russia is actively preparing for a military revival. History often repeats itself.

When Hitler attacked Russia in 1941, her military machine was antiquated, she had not recovered from Stalin's brutal purges of the 1930s. Yet she defeated the greatest war machine of the last century. Is Putin ordained to repeat this – or is he a front for a more sinister power?

For many years I have said that in Russia, communism was not the real problem – there has been a demonic spirit *(prince)*, in control of Russia for 800 years.[1]

CHAPTER 3

The War of Gog and Magog

Russia will join with the Arabs

We know that prophecy indicates that Russia will join with the Arabs, not destroy them! She will make the Arabs her allies in a strategic invasion of the Middle East to alter the balance of power.

This is what the Sovereign Lord says: I am against you, O Gog, chief prince of Meshech and Tubal...

After many days you will be called to arms. In future years you will invade a land that has recovered from war, whose people were gathered from many nations to the mountains of Israel, which had long been desolate. They had been brought out from the nations, and now all of them live in safety.

You and all your troops and the many nations with you will go up, advancing like a storm; you will be like a cloud covering the land...

You will come from your place in the far north, you and many nations with you, all of them riding on horses, a great horde, a mighty army.

(Ezekiel 38:3,8-9,15)

Russian Invasion of Israel

To set the scene for the Russian invasion of Israel, we need to remember there will be a ***Revived Roman Empire,*** and the Antichrist will be in Power. This will be a shaky world government that will last for a period of only three-and-a-half years.

When the rapture of the Church takes place, the restraining power of the Holy Spirit ceases to function in the manner that it does now as described in 2 Thessalonians 2:1-10.

Concerning the coming of our Lord Jesus Christ and our being gathered to him, we ask you, brothers, not to become easily unsettled or alarmed by some prophecy, report or letter supposed to have come from us, saying that the day of the Lord has already come. Don't let anyone deceive you in any way, for (that day will not come) until the rebellion occurs and the man of lawlessness is revealed, the man doomed to destruction. He will oppose and will exalt himself over everything that is called God or is worshipped, so that he sets himself up in God's temple, proclaiming himself to be God.

Don't you remember that when I was with you I used to tell you these things? And now you know what is holding him back, so that he may be revealed at the proper time.

For the secret power of lawlessness is already at work; but the one who now holds it back will continue to do so till he is taken out of the way. And then the lawless one will be revealed, whom the Lord Jesus will overthrow with the breath of his mouth and destroy by the splendour of his coming. The coming of the lawless one will be in accordance with the work of Satan displayed in all kinds of counterfeit miracles, signs and wonders, and in every sort of evil that deceives those who are perishing. They perish because they refused to love the truth and so be saved.

When the Church is gone, all hell will break loose on the earth. Dr. Lewis in his book, *"Prophecy 2000,"* says at this time, "Antichrist comes forward and becomes the ruler of the ten nations of the Roman Empire revived in our times. One of the diabolical actions of the Antichrist as he comes to power shortly after the rapture is that he will force a covenant or treaty upon the nation of Israel.

Seven Years of Tribulation

It is this event alone that marks the time parameters of the period we know as the seven years of Tribulation, a time of global trauma. The *covenant signing* marks the beginning of the seven years *(see Daniel 9:24-27)*. The Antichrist will reign over the ten nations and perhaps over other areas as well for the first three-and-a-half years of the seven year Tribulation."

This then is *"The Time Set"* that the prophet Ezekiel spoke about, of a great invasion against the land of Israel. The account of this is found in Ezekiel 38-39. Dr. Lewis says, "We find that the invasion out of the land that is to the extreme north of Israel takes place at a time when Israel is at rest and has peace. That certainly does not describe the condition that exists in the Middle East at the present time.

It is apparent, therefore, that the *Magog-Russian invasion of Israel* will take place during the first three-and-a-half years of the Tribulation when Israel enjoys the protection of the New United Europe. This Magog battle could not be in the last three-and-a-half years because the Antichrist will defile the temple, an event that is referred to by Daniel and Jesus as the abomination of desolation *(Daniel 9:24; Matthew 24:15-22)*.

The Apostle Paul also refers to this event in 2 Thessalonians 2:3,4, where he describes the man of sin entering the temple of God and declaring himself to be divine. When this abomination of desolation has been accomplished, there will be a time of unprecedented trouble for the Jewish people."[1]

Identifying Magog as Russia

Over two dozen Jewish and Christian scholars and writers identify Magog as Russia. The name *"Gog"* is a prophetic name applied by the bible to *the leader of Magog, the nation of Russia.*

Flavius Josephus, writing in the first century, claimed Magog was connected to the Scythian people who lived north of the Black Sea. As G. Rawlinson wrote in his *"Five Great Monarchies"* *(Assyria: Chap 9, footnote)*: *"The Scythians proper of Herodotus and Hippocrates extend from the Danube and the Carpathians on the one side, to the Tanais or Don upon the other."*[2]

This geographic area of the Scythians is the land of ancient southern Russia. The prophet Ezekiel used the ancient tribal name Magog *(from Genesis 10:2)* to identify the geographical location where the leadership of the prophesied invasion would originate.

The well respected scholar of biblical languages, Gesenius, in his definitive *"Hebrew and Chaldee Lexicon"* identified Magog as follows: *"A region, and a great and powerful people of the same name, inhabiting the extreme recesses of the north, who are at sometime to invade the Holy Land (Ezekiel 38, 39). We are to understand just the same nations as the Greeks comprised under the name of Scythians (Joseph. Arch. 1.6,-1)."*

Magog is referred to by Gesenius as being a real nation, a people who will actually invade Israel in the future. Also Gesenius' comment on *"Gog"* treats him as a real *"prince of the land of Magog... also of Rossi, Moschi and Tibareni, who is to come with great forces from the extreme north (Ezekiel 38:15; 39:2), after the Exile (Ezekiel 38:8,12) to invade the Holy Land, and to perish there, as prophesied by Ezekiel."*[3]

Prepare yourself and be ready, you and all your companies that are gathered about you; and be a guard for them... Then you will come from your place out of the far north,

you and many peoples with you, all of them riding on horses, a great company and a mighty army.
(Ezekiel 38:7,15 NKJV)

Russia the Arms Supplier

Jeffrey says, "Aside from Russia, it would be difficult to name any other nation to the far north of Israel that is capable of leading a huge confederacy of nations from Africa, Asia, Eastern Europe and the Middle East against Israel. Furthermore, Russia is the arms supplier to every one of these nations.

They all use Russian AK-47 rifles, T-72 tanks, missiles, and personnel carriers. For the last four decades Russia has trained the military officers and intelligence staff of all of the nations listed in Ezekiel's prophecy. The phrase *'Prepare yourself'* and *'be a guard for them'* may indicate Russia's future role in providing arms and military leadership to the huge confederacy of nations."[4]

After the invasion of Israel by Russia, *(Russia - lose)* according to the prophecy in the book of Daniel, there will be a time lapse of about three-and-half years, a time when the Jews rebuild the Temple *(Revelation 11:1-2)*.

CHAPTER 4

The Rapture of the Church

Caught Up

The promise of the rapture is the blessed hope and joy of the Church.

For the Lord Himself will descend from heaven with a shout, with the voice of an archangel, and with the trumpet of God. And the dead in Christ shall rise first. Then we who are alive and remain shall be caught up together with them in the clouds to meet the Lord in the air. And thus we shall always be with the Lord.

(1 Thessalonians 4:16-17 NKJV)

The word rapture appears in the bible in the original Greek word *"harazo,"* which is translated, *"caught up."*

The question for many of us is — When will it be?

Christ promised that the saints who *"believe in Me"* who are living when He returns *"shall never die" (John 11:26 KJV).* He prophesied that there will be living saints who *"believe in Me"* at the time of His return who will *"never die."* Those Christians living when Jesus returns will be the first generation of saints that will never experience death. Their unique destiny is that they will pass from ***"life to life eternal."***

We need to remember that the church or the *"called,"* *"chosen"* and *"faithful"* identify with the true Church — the body of Christ. Those who are religious, which have a form of godliness but deny the power thereof *(2 Timothy 3:5)* will not be raptured. They substitute religious rights and membership for true repentance and salvation. God considers all people who worship anyone or anything besides Himself participants in spiritual fornication and adultery. He includes even those who are sincere in their involvement.

The overcomers are all the people who are born-again, who know Jesus as their personal Saviour.

> *For whatsoever is born of God overcometh the world: and this is the victory that overcometh the world, even our faith. Who is he that overcometh the world, but he that believeth that Jesus is the Son of God?*
>
> *(1 John 5:4-5 KJV)*

Everyone who is saved has overcome the world by the grace of God, He is no longer in darkness but in the light.

New Resurrection Bodies

The real purpose of the rapture is to gather together and *"translate"* all the members of the Church, living and departed, into their new resurrection bodies to live with Christ forever. If we are to rule with Christ on the earth and enjoy all that God has prepared for us in heaven we must have a resurrection body.

When a Christian dies his soul is transferred instantly to heaven in the spirit while his body is said to *"rest"* in the ground. Jesus told the thief on the cross, *"Today you will be with Me in paradise"* (Luke 23:43).

When Paul talked about being *"absent from the body and to be present with the Lord"* (2 Corinthians 5:8 NKJV), he confirmed that, at death, our spirits go immediately to heaven. The moment a Christian dies, their spirit is taken to heaven where they will dwell with Christ and the other departed saints until the rapture when they will receive their new spiritual bodies. The apostle Paul and hundreds of millions of departed saints are in heaven today in their spirit without their bodies. They eagerly await the day of the rapture so that they can receive their glorious resurrection bodies.

As Paul tells us in Romans 8:22-23, *"For we know that the whole creation groans with pangs until now. And not only they, but we also who have the first fruits of the Spirit, even we ourselves groan within ourselves, eagerly waiting for the adoption, the redemption of our body."*

Finally, in their new resurrection bodies, they will enjoy the Marriage Supper of the Lamb. Then, in their glorious new bodies, the saints will *"rule and reign"* with Christ on earth forever.

At the moment of the rapture all Christians, including the living saints as well as the departed saints whose souls are in heaven, will instantly receive their new spiritual resurrection body. This body will be identical in nature to the body of Christ after He rose from the dead two thousand years ago.

Philippians 3:21 *(NKJV)* tells us that Christ,

> *Will transform our lowly body that it may be conformed to His glorious body, according to the working by which He is able even to subdue all things to Himself.*

Spiritual Bodies Immortal

At the glorious moment of rapture all members of Christ's true Church, living and dead, will be instantly transformed into their spiritual bodies that will be immortal, indestructible, and able to travel at the speed of thought, just as Jesus did after His resurrection.

When Christ descends from heaven to meet the raptured Christians, the spirits of all of the departed saints will descend in the clouds with Him to be joined to their new resurrection bodies that will rise to meet them.

As Paul assured us, *"For if we believe that Jesus died and rose again, even so God will bring with Him those who sleep in*

Jesus" (1 Thessalonians 4:14 NKJV). This includes departed Christians of varying levels of personal holiness; it is obvious that our participation in the rapture does not depend on our degree of personal sanctification. After all, we have no righteousness of our own, only the *"righteousness of God"* in Christ *(2 Corinthians 5:21)*.

If we are truly *"born again"* we will receive our resurrection body at the rapture with the rest of the millions of Christian saints who have followed Jesus during the last two thousand years. The Lord will reward individual saints for their personal walk with Christ by giving rewards and crowns at the judgement seat of Christ following the rapture.

David Allen Lewis says, "Understanding the rapture teaching of the bible does not insure you against all physical suffering or persecution, but it does insure that no false second coming of a *'christ'* that is not Jesus Christ will ever fool you.

There could be several such events, given the fact that the New Age leadership has a number of *'christ candidates.'* You must understand that before the real Jesus stands on the Mount of Olives, fulfilling the Zechariah prophecy, there is an event involving you personally. I refer to the *'catching away'* of the living believers, *'our gathering together unto Him'* (2 Thessalonians 2:1) when He *'receives us unto Himself.'*

In short I refer to the glorious rapture of the Church! You will hear His trumpet and victory shout. You will rise to meet Him in the air. Hello, Jesus! I know it is really You!

Pre-Tribulation Rapture

The pre-tribulation rapture is no guarantee that there will not be pre-rapture tribulation for some of us. The rapture provides an escape from the seven years' tribulation for only a portion of the Church — those who are alive at the time of the event.

The understanding of the rapture concept makes you deception-proof in relation to the major end-time satanic delusion, the false second coming. *First* will come the rapture of the Church, the catching away. This is followed by the seven years of global trauma, the Tribulation.

After the seven years the visible, manifest coming of Christ takes place. This is when He stands on the Mount of Olives. This marks the beginning, not of a humanistic New Age of Aquarius, but the glorious Millennium *(thousand years)*, the reign of our Saviour, the real Jesus Christ our Eternal Lord.

This Millennium is not an end, but a beginning, for it inaugurates the eternal Kingdom of God which ultimately includes a new heaven and a new earth wherein righteousness eternally dwells."[1]

Under the Reign of the Beast

No portion of the born-again church will have to undergo the specific seven years of God's wrath known as the *"Tribulation"* — the time of global sorrows and outpoured judgements. The Church will not live under the reign of the beast *(Antichrist)*.

Behold, I tell you a mystery: We shall not all sleep, but we shall all be changed; in a moment, in the twinkling of an eye, at the last trumpet. For the trumpet will sound, and the dead will be raised incorruptible, and we shall be changed.

(1 Corinthians 15:51-52 NKJV)

In this passage Paul reveals details of the sequence of events at the glorious rapture.

Paul knew that Christ could delay His return for thousands of years, but he also knew that He might return to rapture His saints at any time, from the days of the early church until today. Paul's hope to participate in the rapture indicates that Christ's return for His Church is imminent.

It seems also that John had the same *"imminent"* hopes of the rapture, when warning against the Antichrist.

Dear children, this is the last hour; and as you have heard that the antichrist is coming, even now many antichrists have come. This is how we know it is the last hour. They went out from us, but they did not really belong to us. For if they had belonged to us they would have remained with us; but their going showed that none of them belonged to us.

But you have an anointing from the Holy One, and all of you know the truth. I do not write to you because you do not know the truth, but because you do know it and because no lie comes from the truth. Who is the liar? It is the man who denies that Jesus is the Christ. Such a man is the antichrist — he denies the Father and the Son.

No one who denies the Son has the Father; whoever acknowledges the Son has the Father also.
(1 John 2:18-23)

Note: The *Funk and Wagnalls Standard Dictionary* defines *"imminent"* as follows: *"about to happen: impending: overhanging as if about to fall; threatening; signifies liable to happen at once, as some calamity, dangerous and close to hand."*

Throughout the New Testament the passages dealing with the return of Christ express the need for watchfulness in light of His imminent return. While Paul longed for the rapture and commanded us to *"wait for His Son from heaven"* he never declared that the resurrection must occur within his lifetime. We should emulate Paul's attitude of watching expectantly for the Lord's return but refuse to set a date for it.

Misguided Predictions

Unfortunately a certain number of people, perhaps well meaning but certainly misguided people have predicted that Jesus would rapture the Church on September 11th, 12th or 13th 1988. One propagator of this era went, apparently as far as to say that if Jesus did not return by the thirteenth it was not because his calculations were wrong, but because the bible is wrong. It must be noted that ***date setting is forbidden*** in the scripture *(Matthew 24:36,44; 25:13; Mark 13:32-33)*.

No one knows about that day or hour, not even the angels in heaven, nor the Son, but only the Father. Be on guard! Be alert! You do not know when that time will come.
(Mark 13:32-33)

The rapture itself is a first stage of the Second Coming of Christ that will ultimately end with His revelation in glory at Armageddon. However until then, Christ is *"Our Blessed Hope"* and we must not be tainted with a lifestyle of irresponsibility.

We are to *"occupy till He comes."*

CHAPTER 5

The Great Tribulation

Seven Years are Divided

The Tribulation is the seven-year period falling between the rapture of the Church and the Second Advent of Jesus Christ to the earth. It is the concluding period of Daniel's prophecy of 70 weeks *(Daniel 9:24-27)*. The seven years are divided into two equal periods, the latter being called the Great Tribulation *(Matthew 24:21)*.

The character of the period is clearly revealed in scripture.

It is a time of:

- *Wrath*   *Zephaniah 1:15-18; 1 Thessalonians 1:10; 5:9; Revelation 6:16-17; 11:18; 14:10,19; 15:1,7; 19:15*

- *Indignation*   *Isaiah 26:20-21; 34:1-3*
- *Trial*   *Revelation 3:10*
- *Trouble*   *Jeremiah 30:7; Zephaniah 1:14-15;*
                  Daniel 12:1
- *Destruction*   *Joel 1:15; 1 Thessalonians 5:3*
- *Darkness*   *Joel 2:2; Amos 5:18; Zephaniah 1:14-18*
- *Desolation*   *Daniel 9:27; Zephaniah 1:14-15*
- *Overturning*   *Isaiah 24:1-4, 19-21*
- *Punishment*   *Isaiah 24:20-21*

Two Main Purposes Stated for the Tribulation

First: God will prepare a believing remnant in the nation Israel to whom Messiah will come and in whom all Israel's covenants will be fulfilled. The gospel of the Kingdom, the good news that The King is coming, will be preached universally *(Matthew 24:14)*, and multitudes will accept by faith the offered salvation. God will again do for Israel what He did through John the Baptist at the first advent *(Matthew 3:1-10; Luke 3:3-14 cf. Malachi 4:5-6)*.

Second: God will pour out His judgement upon unbelieving men and nations *(Revelation 3:10; Jeremiah 25:32-33; Isaiah 24:1; 1 Thessalonians 2:16)*. These judgements will fall both directly from God and indirectly through men and armies.

There is no doubt that the greatest destruction in all history of mankind is still to come, that time is the great Tribulation. The Church however is not mentioned specifically within the prophecies concerning the Tribulation period.

When *"saints"* or *"elect"* are mentioned, regarding persecution during the Tribulation period, in a close examination we discover the references are of the Jewish or Gentile believers who will become followers of God following the rapture of the Church.

The Time of Jacob's Trouble

The demonstration of Satan's evil intention to destroy mankind is the purpose of the Tribulation. The prophet Jeremiah calls it *"the time of Jacob's trouble"* because it will be a time of refining and purifying for God's chosen People *(those who respond during the Tribulation period)*. In addition, God will pour out His wrath on the sinful Gentiles of that day who will joyfully worship the Antichrist and kill the Tribulation saints.

During the terrible time of persecution following the rapture of the Church, God will turn to Israel and call out the 144,000 Jews *"a light unto the gentiles."*

In Revelation 7:3 an angel is held back from pouring out the judgements of God until 144,000 Jewish witnesses are sealed for supernatural protection.

"Sealed" by the angels,

Then I saw another angel ascending from the east, having the seal of the Living God. And he cried with a loud voice to the four angels to whom it was granted to harm the earth and the sea, saying, "Do not harm the earth, the sea, or the trees till we have sealed the servants of our God on their foreheads."

(Revelation 7:2-3 NKJV)

Throughout the bible we see that God always differentiates between the righteous and the unrighteous in terms of His wrath and judgement. The Lord never pours out His wrath upon the righteous.

To prove His righteous judgement, God will hold back the angels that are prepared to pour out the judgements to "*harm*" the earth and sea until they place the divine protection of the seal of God.

Three Different Groups

God promises He will never leave this world without a witness to His truth. After the rapture of the Church the Lord will send three different groups to witness and preach repentance during the great Tribulation. Revelation tells us that these messengers include the two witnesses and finally, three angelic messengers to warn men to repent of their wicked rebellion and seek the face of God.

God's mercy endures forever. Through His divine order, He keeps the gospel steadily flowing to all the earth. Salvation is still available through believing the gospel, the power of God unto salvation *(Romans 1:16)*.

The angelic ministry is extremely diverse. While some angels are preaching the everlasting gospel to all nations, others are announcing the destruction of the Babylonian harlot religious system.

Then I saw another angel flying in midair, and he had the eternal gospel to proclaim to those who live on the earth — to every nation, tribe, language and people. He said in a loud voice, "Fear God and give him glory, because the hour of his judgement has come. Worship him who made the heavens, the earth, the sea and the springs of water." A second angel followed and said, "Fallen! Fallen is Babylon the Great, which made all the nations drink the maddening wine of her adulteries."

(Revelation 14:6-8)

These angels announce to the world that the Antichrist led his armies in the harlot's destruction to make way for the fulfilment of his own evil ambition to become God.

Greatest Harvest of Souls

Though **this time will be the most horrifying time of judgement in history,** hundreds of millions of men and women from every nation will respond to the preaching of the *"gospel of the kingdom"* and will turn from there sinful rebellion against God.

In Revelation 7:9 John tells us of,

A great multitude which no one could number, of all nations, tribes, peoples and tongues.

Later the angel tells John that,

These are the ones who come out of the great tribulation, and washed their robes and made them white in the blood of the Lamb.

(Revelation 7:14 NKJV)

The fact is that the Tribulation period will produce the greatest harvest of souls in world history, the tragic thing is it will be in a harvest of blood. It is said that the vast majority of those who accept Christ during the Tribulation will become martyrs when they reject the false worship of the Babylonian church or the Mark of the Beast.

It is probable that only a small remnant will survive till Armageddon to be supernaturally delivered by the angels when,

"One will be taken and the other left."

CHAPTER 6

The Valley of Decision

The Battle of Armageddon

Multitudes, multitudes in the valley of decision! For the day of the Lord is near in the valley of decision *(Joel 3:14 NKJV).* Israel is for us the key nation to watch if we want to understand the unfolding plans of God, in redeeming the earth. The prophet Joel prophesied the coming great day of the Lord, when God will bring the nations to meet Israel in *"the valley of decision."*

The battle that has been appointed will occur in the great Valley of Jezreel, in the northern part of Israel, that lies before the ancient city of Megiddo. *This Battle of Armageddon is to determine who will rule the world.*

The prophet Joel declared,

> *Proclaim this among the nations: "Prepare for war! Wake up the mighty men, let all the men of war draw near, let them come up. Beat your plowshares into swords and your pruning hooks into spears."*
>
> *(Joel 3:9-10 NKJV)*

The later years of the Tribulation, which is referred, to as the Great Tribulation will be marked by a series of terrifying wars as many nations rebel against the Antichrist.

When the Antichrist gains victory over the Babylonian church his armies will then be concentrated in Europe and the Middle East.

> *I saw three unclean spirits like frogs coming out of the mouth of the dragon, out of the mouth of the beast, and out of the mouth of the false prophet.*
>
> *For they are spirits of demons, performing signs, which go out to the kings of the earth and out of the whole world, to gather them to the battle of that great day of God Almighty... And they gathered them together to the place called in Hebrew; Armageddon.*
>
> *(Revelation 16:13-14, 16 NKJV)*

The Gathering of Kings

These *"unclean spirits"* will call the *"Kings of the earth"* to gather their armies to Israel for the final conflict of the age. First the king of the South *(Egypt and her allies)* will attack the Antichrist's forces in Israel. Then the king of the North

(Russia, Syria) will join the invasion by bringing his forces down from the north in a lightening attack.

> *At the time of the end the king of the South shall attack him; and the king of the North shall come against him like a whirlwind, with chariots, horseman, and with many ships.*
>
> *(Daniel 11:40 NKJV)*

Antichrist and his armies fight back and in so doing totally annihilate them. Daniel prophesied that, *"He shall enter the countries, overwhelm them, and pass through."*

The Antichrist will command the support of most western nations led by his inner circle of Ten European and Mediterranean nations. He will consolidate his military forces in Israel knowing that the final war will be fought in the Promised Land.

> *He shall also enter the Glorious Land, and many countries shall be overthrown; but these shall escape from his hand: Edom, Moab, and the prominent people of Ammon. He shall stretch out his hand against the countries, and the land of Egypt shall not escape.*
>
> *(Daniel 11:41-42 NKJV)*

The armies of the Antichrist will conquer Israel and Egypt. Daniel tells us that Edom, Moab and Ammon in present-day Jordan will escape. Possibly, they are willing allies of Satan's prince. The Antichrist will conquer Libya and Ethiopia as his armies consolidate his control over North Africa.

> *But news from the East and the North shall trouble him; therefore he shall go out with great fury to destroy and*

annihilate many. And he shall plant the tents of his palace between the seas and the gloriously holy mountain; yet he shall come to his end, and no one will help him.

(Daniel 11:44-45 NKJV)

At the moment of his triumph over these rebellious nations the Antichrist will receive intelligence reports that an enormous army is mobilising far to the East and North. These reports will greatly disturb him because the army of *"the Kings of the East"* will contain **two hundred million soldiers.**

The Armies Gather

The pouring of the sixth vial directly relates to the sounding of the sixth trumpet of Revelation 9.

And the sixth angel poured out his vial upon the great river Euphrates; and the water thereof was dried up, that the way of the kings of the east might be prepared.

(Revelation 16:12 KJV)

The Trumpet is Blown

The sixth trumpet releases the vast demon-driven Oriental army. To reach its destination, the battle site of Armageddon, it marches through the Asian areas, destroying everything in its path.

The Euphrates River has stood as a great river and is the largest river in Western Asia, its source being central Armenia formed by the junction in Asia Minor of the Kara-su and Murad-su Rivers, from which it pursues a south-easterly course to the Persian Gulf. It is about 1,800 miles long.

The overflow of the Euphrates and the use of canals as in Egypt made possible bountiful crops that at one time sustained a large population. Since the Mongolian and Mohammedan conquests, the land has been mostly unproductive, but now the Iraq government is restoring the canals and building dams.

Also the massive Ataturk Dam was completed in Turkey which caused the Euphrates River to drop in level by 75%. Now for the first time in history any invading armies can easily cross this great river.

That army is a vast incredible 200 million man eastern army that will need to reach its prophesied destination. *"The Battle of Armageddon."* This battle will be at Megiddo, many major battles have been fought in the Valley of Megiddo, and it has been the site of over 12,000 battles in six thousand years!

Mount Megiddo is approximately 56 miles from Jerusalem. Because of its strategic location lying on the north side of the Carmel ridge and commanding the strategic pass between the coastal plain and the valley of Esdraelon... Mount Megiddo sits next to the plain of Jezreel, which extends from the Mediterranean to the Jordan.

In this great valley, hundreds of millions will die in bloody warfare as the advanced dooms-day weapons are finally taken out of the armoires to slaughter the nations. Nothing will be held back as the nations unleash total destruction on their enemies and cities. A full scale nuclear, biological and chemical war could destroy over 90% of the population in the countries attacked.

The devastation will be so overwhelming the survivors may envy the dead.

Nature's Final Upheaval

And the seventh angel poured out his vial into the air; and there came a great voice out of the temple of heaven, from the throne, saying, "It is done."

(Revelation 16:17 KJV)

As the Tribulation comes to an end, the seventh angel pours his vial into the air as the pronouncement comes from heaven *"It is done."* This signals the sounding of the seventh trumpet. This is the same event as the angel's declaration in Revelation 10:7 *(KJV).*

But in the days of the voice of the seventh angel, when he shall begin to sound, the mystery of God should be finished, as he hath declared to his servants the prophets.

Suddenly the most tremendous upheaval of nature ever to occur begins. This is the cataclysmic event, which follows Jesus' opening of the sixth seal *(Revelation 6)* and the sounding of the final trumpet *(Revelation 11).*

And there were voices, and thunders, and lightnings; and there was a great earthquake, such as was not since men were upon the earth, so mighty an earthquake, and so great.

And the great city was divided into three parts, and the cities of the nations fell: and great Babylon came in remembrance before God, to give unto her the cup of the wine of the fierceness of his wrath. And every island fled away, and the mountains were not found.

And there fell upon men a great hail out of heaven, every stone about the weight of a talent: and men blasphemed God because of the plague of the hail; for the plague thereof was exceeding great.

(Revelation 16:18-21 KJV)

Babylonian Beast System

God remembers Babylon, the total Babylonian Beast System used by the Antichrist, and pours out the fierceness of His wrath. The upheaval is so devastating that the entire surface of the earth changes. As the earthquake destroys the land, **hail weighing** a talent *(approximately **120 pounds**)* falls from heaven. This upheaval could easily bring about the fulfilment of Isaiah 13:13 which states, the earth shall remove out of her place.

Coagulated Blood fills the Atmosphere

Hilton Sutton says, "Imagine the terrible scene. The stench of the oceans' coagulated blood fills the atmosphere. The rays of the sun are hot, and no water is available to drink — only blood! The people who have taken the mark of the beast and worshipped his image are troubled with boils and, of course, raging fever.

On this final day of Tribulation, people are suffering from the last plagues, the great earthquake and hail stones, the return of Christ to the earth, and the monumental Battle of Armageddon."[1]

Then the beast was captured, and with him the false prophet who worked signs in his presence, by which he deceived those who received the mark of the beast and those who worshipped his image. These two were cast alive into the lake of fire burning with brimstone. And the rest were killed with the sword, which proceeded from the mouth of Him who sat on the horse. And all the birds were filled with their flesh *(Revelation 19:20-21)*.

Christ Descends

When Christ descends on the Mount of Olives to defeat the armies of Satan, He will enter the rebuilt Temple through the sealed Eastern Gate. This gate often called the Golden Gate, guards the entrance to the Temple on the eastern wall of the Temple Mount.

Jesus will cross the Kidron Valley past His beloved Garden of Gethsemane to approach the sealed Eastern Gate. Ezekiel 43:1-5 foretold the coming of the Messiah to His Temple:

> *Behold, the glory of the God of Israel came from the way of the east. His voice was like the sound of many waters; and the earth shone with His glory... And the glory of the Lord came into the Temple by way of the gate which faces toward the east.*
>
> *(Ezekiel 43:2,4 NKJV)*

He is proclaimed **Lord of lords, King of kings, and the Prince of Peace** *(Isaiah 9:6)*. Then He begins His Wonderful 1,000-year reign of peace and righteousness on earth.

CHAPTER 7

The Millennium

The Thousand Years

The Millennium is only mentioned six times, all in Revelation 20. This word comes from the Latin mille, *"a thousand,"* and annum, *"year," "a thousand years,"* and is a theological term based upon the thousand years spoken of in Revelation 20:2-7. A thousand-year reign of the Messiah is also the concept of a number of Jewish rabbinical scholars.

The Presbyterian scholar Nathaniel West in his book *"The Thousand Years"* has cited some of these:

- Rabbi Eleasar said, *"Messiah's Days shall be 1,000 years..."*

- Elias, a Doctor of the Second Temple, and the School of Elias, both say *"Messiah's Kingdom is 1,000 years..."*

- Rabbi Qatina and Rabbi Jose say the same, adding that *"Messiah's Days are the Days of Restitution for Israel, and are a 1,000 years"*[1]

David Allen Lewis in his book, *"Prophecy 2000"* says, "It should be pointed out that the Millennium is not the kingdom of God. The kingdom of God is eternal. The Millennium is a physical, earthly demonstration of the kingdom of God.

The Millennium is an ideal age, not a perfect age. Perfection awaits the eternity that follows the Millennium. People will have children, and those children will have to choose to accept or reject Jesus Christ. People will still rebel; there will be punishment, for Christ will rule with a rod of iron *(Isaiah 65:20; Zechariah 14:16-19; Revelation 19:15; Psalms 2:9).*

Because Jesus reigns, it will be a time of unprecedented blessing, prosperity, and peace. War and crime will not be tolerated and Satan will be bound.

Because people will be born and salvation will be a necessity, the Holy Spirit's work continues. There will be an outpouring of the Holy Spirit as the greater fulfilment of Joel 2:28 takes place."[2]

The Meaning of the Millennium

Herman Hoyt speaks of the spiritual nature of the Millennium:

"Basically the kingdom will be spiritual in nature. Meaning that it belongs to and is governed by the Spirit of God. It possesses every tangible and material quality of a real kingdom, and these under the control and direction of the Holy Spirit. Forgiveness, direct knowledge of God *(Jeremiah 31:34)*; righteousness *(Jeremiah 23:5-6)*; spiritual cleansing *(Ezekiel 36:24-26)*; and regeneration *(Ezekiel 36:26-28)*; will all be present.

The fruit of spiritual control will be manifest in ethical conduct... religious purification ...and the Shekinah glory will again take up its rightful place in the Temple *(Ezekiel 43:1-7)*. The original intention of God for Israel will be accomplished in this people becoming the leaders and teachers of religious truth *(Isaiah 61:6).*"[3]

Praise God the Antichrist is not the star of the end-time drama. The central figure of the Millennium is the Lord Jesus Christ. In his book, ***"The Holy Spirit," L. Thomas Holdcroft*** writes:

"At the revelation of Jesus Christ, the divine Son of David; ...will at last assume His place as King of kings. The Holy Spirit will suitably anoint and empower Him for His role; 'There shall come forth a rod out of the stem of Jesse... And the Spirit of the Lord shall rest upon him...' *(Isaiah 11:1-2 KJV)* It may be said that the governing skill of the divine Christ will be exercised in and through the Holy Spirit."[4]

Of the Messiah Isaiah writes, "Behold my servant, whom I uphold; mine elect in whom my soul delighteth; I have put my spirit upon him: he shall bring forth judgement to the Gentiles" *(Isaiah 42:1 KJV)*.

There Will Be Literal Sacrifices

Dr Lewis says that, "The objection that the sacrifices in the millennial temple are unnecessary and redundant has always puzzled me. First of all, Ezekiel says, there will be sacrifices.

I know of no other author who claims that the sacrifices have any redemptive value. Indeed, every author that I know of, who treats the subject from a literalist point of view states clearly that the sacrifices are commemorative of the Lord's death as the Communion commemorates His death. The sacrifices are necessary as a reminder of the awful price that was paid for the salvation of all who believe in Him."[5]

The blessed Holy Spirit is ever the director of our worship to the Lord Jesus Christ. In *"The Spirit Himself,"* R.M. Riggs wrote:

"As our present baptism in the Spirit, walk in the Spirit, and knowledge of the Spirit are but a foretaste of the fullness, which awaits us at the coming of our Lord and Saviour, so the whole work and ministry of the Spirit on the earth in this dispensation are but drops of blessing compared with the great, sweeping, universal work that is before Him during the Millennium.

Christ in person and the Holy Spirit in immanent presence work hand in hand in the reclamation and transformation of the earth in this period... the Holy Spirit will then have full and free sway among the sons of men. Then shall Joel's prophecy find its full fulfilment... This will be a grand climax of the work of the Holy Spirit. To pervade the earth with His presence, to teach men to glorify the Lord... to bring all things into subjection to Christ — these are His great objectives, and the thousand years of peace will witness His complete attainment of these great ends."[6]

The Saints Rule with Jesus

In Revelation 20:4, we read, "I saw thrones on which were seated those who had been given authority to judge. And I saw the souls of those who had been beheaded because of their testimony for Jesus and because of the Word of God. They had not worshipped the beast of his image and had not received his mark on their foreheads or their hands. They came to life and reigned with Christ a thousand years."

The members of the Church return with Jesus to administrate His earthly kingdom for one thousand years. During this reign, a theocratic government exists, a perfect administration. There are no political parties, labour unions, or police.

The saints who have returned with Jesus fill all positions of authority from the local level to the highest government official. Remember the resurrected Christian saints will have access to the earth to carry out God's plan to rule His kingdom.

Resurrected Christians will teach those on earth about their need for personal salvation. Throughout the Millennium billions of Gentiles and Jews, born to those who survived the Great Tribulation, will respond to the preaching of the gospel by the resurrected saints. John was given a Vision of the rewards for the martyred saints who paid the supreme price for their faith *(Revelation 20:4)*.

Will Health and Peace Reign?

Satan's imprisonment almost negates his earthly operation. Since he is the only cause of death, sickness, and temptation, these become almost non-existent. Longevity of life is restored to these natural people, who continue to reproduce children.

> *There shall be no more thence an infant of days, nor an old man that hath not filled his days: for the child shall die an hundred years old; but the sinner being an hundred years old shall be accursed.*
>
> *(Isaiah 65:20 KJV)*

We would still be considered a child if one were to die at a 100 years old. Any death during the Millennium results from sin began in unrighteous people before Satan's imprisonment.

The Peace that is brought through the reign of Christ will even extend to all animals. Any creatures turned natural enemies by Adam's fall are reconciled. Parents need not worry about their children. Even if a child should reach into the hole of a serpent, he will not be bitten.

> *The wolf will live with the lamb, the leopard will lie down with the goat, the calf and the lion and the yearling together; and a little child will lead them. The cow will feed with the bear, their young will lie down together, and the lion will eat straw like the ox.*

The infant will play near the hole of the cobra, and the young child put his hand into the viper's nest. They will neither harm nor destroy on all my holy mountain, for the earth will be full of the knowledge of the Lord as the waters cover the sea.

(Isaiah 11:6-9)

Satan's Last Act of Rebellion

Many nations are saved during the Millennium *(Revelation 21:24)*. However, even those who are not saved must worship Jesus during this time *(Zechariah 14:16-17)*. The people who do not receive Jesus as Saviour and Lord have an opportunity to follow Satan when he is released from the bottomless pit at the end of the 1,000-year period. John warned that many will be deceived and join in Satan's final rebellion:

When the thousand years are over, Satan will be released from his prison and will go out to deceive the nations in the four corners of the earth - Gog and Magog - to gather them to battle. In number they are like the sand of the seashore.

(Revelation 20:7-8)

Do not confuse the terms Gog and Magog of Revelation 20 with their use in Ezekiel 38 and 39. In Ezekiel's prophecies Gog and Magog represented a great northern power identifiable as Russia from the geographical areas described. This prophecy of Ezekiel 38 began to be fulfilled with the restoration of the nation of Israel. The Gog and Magog of Revelation 20 are gathered together from all over the earth and are destroyed.

The Final Rebellion

"Incredibly, many citizens of the Millennium will join in this final rebellion against the Messiah. Despite the fact that Jesus will visibly rule from Jerusalem billions will rebel against God when Satan is released from the bottomless pit *'for a season.'*

Perhaps God will test the billions of souls born during the Millennium to prove that, even in a Paradise of peace and justice, without personal salvation and the grace of God, man, when tempted, will always choose sinful rebellion."[7]

God, sends fire from heaven to end this strange battle, moving so swiftly that it is as though the battle never actually occurs. Satan is again taken captive, then cast into the lake of fire where the Antichrist and false prophet have been for 1,000-years. The only people left alive on the earth are the saints from all time periods, the righteous remnant of Israel, and the nations saved during Christ's reign.

This will be Satan's final battle. **One thousand years after Armageddon,** *"The devil, who deceived them, was cast into the lake of fire and brimstone where the beast and the false prophet are. And they will be tormented day and night forever and ever"* (Revelation 20:10 NKJV). Satan will never again be a part of the universe. Hell was created for Satan and his fallen angels as Christ described, *"the everlasting fire prepared for the devil and his angels"* (Matthew 25:41 NKJV).

The Nature Of Life In HELL

Naturally, few people have spent much time considering the nature of life in hell, says Jeffrey. "Even for religious people, the mind recoils from that grim reality. However, since our choice of an eternal destiny in heaven or hell is the most important decision we will ever make, it is worthwhile to consider what the bible reveals about hell.

The horror of hell will consist of an eternity without God, without love or beauty or hope.

The bible calls it the 'Lake of Fire' referring to its physical torment and suffering. Those who go to hell will receive resurrection bodies that can feel pain but cannot die. *'And I saw the dead, small and great, standing before God, and books were opened' (Revelation 20:12 NKJV).*

In Mark 9:43, Christ warned that the body of sinners would never die: One of the worst horrors of hell will be the unrepentant sinners that will share that terrible experience. Most people have never considered who their companions will be in hell if they choose to reject God's mercy.

Sinners sometimes joke that they will meet their friends in hell for a re-union. Those poor souls who have been sentenced to a penitentiary will tell you that the hardened criminals who had no hope of getting out... inflicted unspeakable horrors on new prisoners.

In hell every unrepentant killer, torturer, violent and hateful person in history will share that prison with those average people whose sinful pride prevented them from accepting God's salvation. There will be no guards, bars or laws to protect one prisoner from another. Those violent predators who enjoy tormenting others will have no reason to restrain their evil impulses. And it will never end."[8]

The Great White Throne Judgement

From verse 11 of Revelation 20 the scene changes from earth to the throne room in heaven:

Then I saw a great white throne and him who was seated on it. Earth and sky fled from his presence, and there was no place for them. And I saw the dead, great and small, standing before the throne, and books were opened. Another book was opened, which is the book of life. The dead were judged according to what they had done as recorded in the books.

The sea gave up the dead that were in it, and death and Hades gave up the dead that were in them, and each person was judged according to what he had done. Then death and Hades were thrown into the lake of fire. The lake of fire is the second death. If anyone's name was not found written in the book of life, he was thrown into the lake of fire.

(Revelation 20:11-15)

In this final resurrection, the wicked dead of all ages are resurrected to stand before God's throne. No one is left on earth, and hell is emptied. While this judgement is taking place in heaven, earth and the heavens surrounding earth are destroyed.

God, as judge, sits on one side of the throne. Angels back Him and the righteous overcomers, people of all ages: the Old and New Testament saints, the Tribulation saints, the nations saved during the Millennium, and the godly angels.

Waiting to be judged on the other side all nations, which did not turn to God, slain during the Tribulation or at the Millennium's end, and the fallen angels. Paul refers to these angels in the following verse:

> *And the angels who did not keep their positions of authority but abandoned their own home — these he has kept in darkness, bound with everlasting chains for judgement on the great Day.*
>
> *(Jude 1:6)*

God judges the unrighteous according to their works recorded in the book He opens. Afterwards, He assigns them to their final place of punishment, the lake of fire. This is the second death, a state of eternal death!

Remember the righteous never see the second death.

CHAPTER 8

Jerusalem, A Holy City

A Final Transformation

The Book of Revelation says that after the Messianic Millennium, Jerusalem will receive a final transformation. Then God's plan of redemption will be complete and all of God's promises, from those given to Abraham and onwards, will be fulfilled.

> *Then I saw a new heaven and a new earth, for the first heaven and the first earth had passed away, and there was no longer any sea. I saw the Holy City, the New Jerusalem, coming down out of heaven from God, prepared as a bride beautifully dressed for her husband.*
>
> *(Revelation 21:1-2)*

This is the heavenly hope — eternity; not just the reign of the Messiah, but the state and condition of eternity. Remember only righteous people live on the new earth, the unrighteous people will suffer eternally in the lake of fire:

But the fearful, and unbelieving, and the abominable, and murderers, and whoremongers, and sorcerers, and idolaters, and all liars, shall have their part in the lake which burneth with fire and brimstone: which is the second death.

(Revelation 21:8 KJV)

Once a person recognises his or her need for Jesus and then makes his initial move, he begins overcoming Satan. When his action brings him to the point of accepting Jesus as Saviour and Lord, he has overcome! From then on he overcomes daily as he walks with Jesus. To enable us to successfully overcome, Jesus said, *"My Father and I will abide in you" (John 14:23).*

The Holy Spirit plus the authority of the Word make this reality. Jesus said, *"If ye abide in me, and my words abide in you, ye shall ask what ye will, and it shall be done unto you" (John 15:7 KJV).*

The seven statements made to the overcomers in the letters to the churches follow:

- **To him that overcometh** will I give to eat of the tree of life, which is in the midst of the paradise of God *(Revelation 2:7 KJV)*

- **He that overcometh** shall not be hurt of the second death *(Revelation 2:11 KJV)*

- **To him that overcometh** will I give to eat of the hidden manna, and will give him a white stone, and in the stone a new name written, which no man knoweth saving he that receiveth it *(Revelation 2:17 KJV)*

- **And he that overcometh,** and keepeth my works unto the end, to him will I give power over the nations: And he shall rule them with a rod of iron; as the vessels of a potter shall they be broken to shivers: even as I received of my Father. And I will give him the morning star *(Revelation 2:26-28 KJV)*

- **He that overcometh,** the same shall be clothed in white raiment; and I will not blot out his name out of the book of life, but I will confess his name before my Father, and before his angels *(Revelation 3:5 KJV)*

- **Him that overcometh** will I make a pillar in the temple of my God, and he shall go no more out: and I will write upon him the name of my God, and the name of the city of my God, which is new Jerusalem, which cometh down out of heaven from my God: and I will write upon him my new name *(Revelation 3:12 KJV)*

- **To him that overcometh** will I grant to sit with me in my throne, even as I also overcame, and am set down with my Father in his throne *(Revelation 3:21 KJV)*

Then, when sin, death, all the attributes of this age and all its works are over; when this old earth with its kingdoms and cities is gone, Jerusalem will remain — but in a new form.

The New Jerusalem

And there came unto me one of the seven angels which had the seven vials full of the seven last plagues, and talked with me, saying, Come hither, I will show thee the bride, the Lamb's wife.

And he carried me away in the spirit to a great and high mountain, and shewed me that great city, the holy Jerusalem, descending out of heaven from God, Having the glory of God: and her light was like unto a stone most precious, even like a jasper stone, clear as crystal; And had a wall great and high, and had twelve gates, and at the gates twelve angels, and names written thereon, which are the names of the twelve tribes of the children of Israel:

On the east three gates; on the north three gates; on the south three gates; and on the west three gates. And the wall of the city had twelve foundations, and in them the names of the twelve apostles of the Lamb.
(Revelation 21:9-14 KJV)

The New Jerusalem occupied by God the Father, Jesus the Son, and the body of Christ, the Church. Chronologically, the Wedding of the Lamb and the following Marriage Supper occur during the last four years of the Tribulation. The New Jerusalem comes to rest upon the new earth after the Great White Throne Judgement, which follows the Tribulation and the Millennium.

The Jews will be in Heaven Too

The names of the twelve tribes of Israel are written over the gates of the new, heavenly Jerusalem. God's nature is eternal, His plans are eternal. His city is everlasting and His people are everlasting.

I have loved you with an everlasting love; I have drawn you with loving-kindness.

(Jeremiah 31:3)

Jerusalem and the Jewish people have an everlasting, central place in God's world-wide plan of salvation. They have carried God's revelation through history and administered the service in the Temple. It was the Jews who cared for the Land of Israel, and Jerusalem is their city. Through them the Messiah came, the Son of David, the Great King: and it will be from their city Jerusalem that He will reign in peace and righteousness over the whole earth.

We will see all the promises concerning Jerusalem fulfilled. Jerusalem is the part in the picture that will make it complete, meaningful and beautiful. Thus, it is not strange that the crowning words of the prophetic book of Ezekiel are these:

And the name of the city from that time on will be: The Lord is There.

(Ezekiel 48:35)

John describes the New Jerusalem as it comes down from God in heaven. The city is majestic — beautiful like jasper stone! Clear as crystal! It has a great high wall around it with an angel at each of its twelve gates.

And he that talked with me had a golden reed to measure the city, and the gates thereof, and the wall thereof. And the city lieth foursquare, and the length is as large as the breadth: and he measured the city with the reed, twelve thousand furlongs. The length and the breath and the height of it are equal.

(Revelation 21:15-16 KJV)

The New Jerusalem

Hilton Sutton in his book, **"Revelation"** *(this is a verse by verse study of the book of Revelation)* says that, "The New Jerusalem is 1,500 miles square, not square miles. This is the equivalent of 2,250,000 square miles per level. Los Angeles, the largest American city in land area, covers more than 500 square miles. The New Jerusalem is 1,500 miles north to south, east to west, and 1,500 miles high!"

He says, "If it were placed on the United States, laterally it would fit between the Rocky and Appalachian Mountains; longitudinally, between the Canadian border and the Gulf of Mexico. This is not a country or state, but a city — and it is still 1,000 miles high! ...

This city wall is extremely tall:

And he measured the wall thereof, an hundred and forty and four cubits, according to the measure of a man, that is, of the angel.

(Revelation 21:17 KJV)

One hundred and forty four cubits, approximately 216 feet. The height of the city's wall is equivalent to that of a twenty-two-story building.

Its Elegance:

And the building of the wall of it was of jasper: And the city was pure gold, like unto clear glass. And the foundations of the wall of the city were garnished with all manner of precious stones.

The first foundation was jasper; the second, sapphire; the third, a chalcedony; the fourth, an emerald; the fifth, sardonyx; the sixth, sardius; the seventh, chrysolyte; the eighth, beryl; the ninth, a topaz; the tenth, a chrysoprasus; the eleventh, a jacinth; the twelfth, an amethyst.

And the twelve gates were twelve pearls: every several gate was of one pearl: and the street of the city was pure gold, as it were transparent glass. And I saw no temple therein...

(Revelation 21:18-22 KJV)

Twelve magnificent foundations, each formed from a solid precious stone, support the wall, made of Jasper. Each foundation is garnished with the stones of the other eleven. The city is made of pure gold. Each gate, made of a single pearl, in a wall that runs 1,500 miles in one direction and stands about twenty-two-stories high will be magnificent. The gates will have to be massive in order to fit architecturally. One theologian speculated that each gate will be 100 miles wide."[1]

We'll have to wait and see. I pray we can explore this magnificent city together, if I don't see you before, *"I'll see you there."*

Every Blessing
Alan Pateman

81

CHAPTER 9

Appendix

Is this the generation that will witness the return of Christ? The disciples asked the same question, "Now as He sat on the Mount of Olives, the disciples came to Him privately, saying, *'Tell us, when will these things be? And what will be the sign of Your coming, and of the end of the age?'" (Matthew 24:3 NKJV)*

We can only say this must be significant that thirty-eight prophecies have been fulfilled in our generation, which must point to the Lord's return at any moment.

The Odds of Prophecies being fulfilled in our lifetime:

- The Odds of One prophecy: 1 in 50
- The Odds of Two prophecies: 1 in 2500
- The Odds of Three prophecies: 1 in 125,000

- The Odds of Four prophecies: 1 in 6,25 million
- The Odds of Five prophecies: 1 in 312,5 million
- The Odds of Six prophecies: 1 in 15,6 billion
- The Odds of 38 prophecies being fulfilled in one given life-time is simply GOD!

Here are the Prophecies

The Prophecy:	*The Reference:*
• The Rebirth of Israel, the "fig tree" buds	Matthew 24:32-34
• The Hebrew language recovered	Zephaniah 3:9
• The Ethiopian Jews return to Israel	Zephaniah 3:10
• The Exiles returning to Israel	Ezekiel 37:21
• Israel becomes fertile and blossoms	Isaiah 27:6
• Israel's rainfall increases dramatically	Joel 2:23
• The Roman Empire will revive	Daniel 2:40-44
• Russia rises as a military power	Ezekiel 38:1-12
• The City of Babylon is rebuilt	Isaiah 13:1,6,19
• Iraq is defeated in war in the Gulf	Jeremiah 50:1,9; 51:27
• Preparations for a One World Government	Daniel 7:14; Revelation 13:7
• Financial System depending on numbers not cash	Revelation 13:17-18
• Intra-dermal computer ID chips	Revelation 13:15-18
• Global arms race	Matthew 24:6-7; Joel 3:9
• Worldwide television communications	Revelation 11:9-10
• Israel surrounded by enemy Arab nations	Psalms 83:4-8
• Worldwide famine destroying	Revelation 6:5-6; Matthew 24:7

Appendix

- Deadly pestilence kills one-fourth of earth — Revelation 6:8; Matthew 24:7
- Increasing earthquakes in strange places — Revelation 6:12-15; Matthew 24:7
- An increase in false messiahs — Matthew 24:4-5
- Explosion of false prophets and heresies — Matthew 24:24
- The rise of Anti-Semitism worldwide — Matthew 24:9-10
- Men's hearts failing them in fear — Luke 21:26
- Asia developing 200-million man army — Revelation 9:14-16
- The Euphrates River can be dried up — Revelation 16:12-14
- A military highway across Asia — Revelation 9:14-15; Revelation 16:12-14
- Society accepts perversion and evil as normal — 2 Timothy 3:1-3; Revelation 9:20-21
- Ecological devastation of the planet — Revelation 11:18
- Doomsday weapons threaten earth — Matthew 24:21-22; Joel 2:3
- Plans to rebuild the Temple — Isaiah 2:2-3; Micah 4:1-2; Ezekiel 43:14-15
- Levites and Priests train for Temple service — Ezekiel 43:14-15
- Temple vessels are prepared — Ezekiel 43:14-19
- Preparations for the sacrifice of the Red Heifer — Numbers 19; Ezekiel 36:25
- Jerusalem rebuilt in 9 specific directions — Jeremiah 31:38-40
- Massive increases in wealth and possessions — James 5:3
- Formation of worldwide Apostate Church — Revelation 17
- Israel dwelling without walls or gates — Ezekiel 38:11
- The powers of uranium shaken; elements melt — Luke 21:26; 2 Peter 3:10-12

❖

Word Study

Word	*Meaning*
• Abomination:	A person or thing that is disgusting or loathsome - an action which is vicious, vile etc.
• Alchemy:	The pseudoscientific predecessor of chemistry that sought a method to prolong the life of base metals - 2) A power like as above: her beauty had a potent alchemy.
• Allegory:	System of interpretation, which denies literal meaning of the text. Allows one to make the bible mean almost anything.
• Amillennial:	The theory that there will be no literal Millennium or that we are in the Millennium now. The prophetic passages of the bible are spiritualised. There is a wide variety of interpretations among the amillennialists.
• Anthropologist:	The study of man, his origins, institutions, religious beliefs, and social relationships.
• Antichrist:	A literal person. A humanisation, who will rule over ten nations *(Revived Roman*

Empire) for three and a half years, then over a loose world coalition of nations for another three and a half years.

- Antichrist Spirit: Bible - the antagonist of Christ excepted by early Christians to appear and reign over the world until overthrown at Christ's Second Coming.

- Anti-Semite: One hostile to the Jews; one who persecutes Jews.

- Anti-Semitic: Of or showing Anti-Semitism.

- Anti-Semitism: Hostility, prejudice or persecution against Jews.

- Anti-Zionism: Those who are against the establishment and support of a national Homeland for the Jews in Palestine.

- Apostasy: Abandonment of one's religious faith, party or cause.

- Arable: 1) of land, being or capable of being tilled for production of crops 2) of, relating to or using such land.

- Arteriosclerotic: Hardening of the arteries - a thickening of loss of elasticity of the walls.

- Assimilation: To learn and understand it thoroughly to adjust and be adjusted - to become or cause to become similar - to change.

- Assyrian: An inhabitant of ancient Assyria - extinct Semitic language of the Assyrians.

- Astrological: The activities and characteristics and relative positions of the planets, sun and moon.

- Atrocities:

  1) behaviour or an action that is wicked or ruthless 2) the fact or quality of being atrocious 3) acts of extreme cruelty.

- Babylon:

  (in protestant polemic) The Roman Catholic Church regarded as the seat of luxury and corruption.

- Beast *(The):*

  (Revelation 20:10) thêrión - dangerous animal:- *(venomous wild)* beast.

- Belligerent:

  Marked by readiness to fight or argue aggressive - a person or country engaged in war.

- Box Tree:

  A slow growing evergreen tree or shrub with small shinny leaves - used for hedges.

- Castor:

  The aromatic secretion of a beaver, used in perfumery and medicine.

- Catholicism:

  Short for R.C. - the beliefs, practices of any Catholic Church.

- Chaldeans:

  (3777) Kesed, a relative of Abraham:- Chesed astrologer *(as if proverbial of that people):-* Chaldeans inhabitants of Chaldea. Also connected with Babylonians.

- Circumvent:

  To evade or go round - to outwit - to encircle.

- Coalesced:

  To unite or come together in one body or mass; merge, fuse, blend - to increase.

- Communion:

  The art of participating in the Eucharist - Spiritual Union, or with nature.

- Confirmation:

  Something that confirms - a rite in several Christian churches that confirms a baptised person in his faith and admits him to full participation in the church.

- Confession: Act of confessing ones faults or crimes - confession of faith.

- Cosmic: Relating to the whole universe; occurring or originating in outer space.

- Covenant: An agreement between two or more persons, which is binding - Also a promise made by God to the Israelites and their commitment to worship Him alone.

- Debauchery: To lead into a life of depraved self-indulgence - to seduce a woman.

- Declivity: A downward slope, especially of the ground.

- Denunciation: Act of denouncing - denunciator.

- Derogatory: Tending or intended to detract, disparage, or belittle, intentionally offensive.

- Desolation: Ruin or devastation, solitary misery: wretchedness.

- Diagnosis: The identification of disease from examination - a thorough analysis of facts or problems in order to gain understanding.

- Dispersion: The separation of - scattered around some central point.

- Divination: The art or practice of discovering future events or unknown things, as though by supernatural powers.

- Doctrines: A creed or body of teachings of a religious, political, or philosophical group or body of principles being taught.

- Dominion: A modern form of postmillennialism with a strong program for conquest, first of the churches, then the world.

Word Study

- Ecclesiastical: Relating to the Christian Church.

- Ecumenical: Of the whole Christian world or Church; Universal, worldwide; relating to unity among Christian churches.

- Ecumenism: Movement seeking to bring unity among Christian churches.

- Eisegesis: Reading meaning into the text, depending on your own preconceived ideas. To insert meaning into text from outside sources.

- El-Shaddai: Translated *"Almighty"* and suggests the all-powerful nature of God. Shaddai is connected with the Hebrew word for breast, and signifies one who nourishes, supplies and satisfies. The one who sheds forth and pours out sustenance and blessing. The concept of abundance is inextricably intertwined with this great name of God.

- Emancipation: To free from restriction or restraint to free from inhibitions of conventional morality - to liberate from bondage.

- Eschatology: Greek: Escha - the end; ology - knowledge of. Hence, the study of the end-time prophecy.

- Exegesis: Seeking the meaning that is inherent in the text. To take out from the text the meaning that is actually there.

- Fables: A short moral story, one with animals as people - false, fictitious - to tell lies.

- Fabrications: To make, build, construct - to fake or forge.

- Fetishes: Something e.g. inanimate object to have magical powers, any object, activity etc, to which one is excessively devoted.

- Flagellation: To whip, flog.

- Freemason: Member of a widespread secret order constituted in London in 1717 - Often shortened to Mason.

- Harlot: Whore, prostitute.

- Hebron: Hebrew (2275) - Chebrôwn, seat of association; Cheron, a place in Palestine also the name of two Israelis. Cheber (2267) a society - a spell - charmer (-ing) - company - enchantment - wide.

- Holocaust: Great destruction or loss of life or the source of such destruction: the mass murder of Jews in Nazi Germany.

- Homogenised: To break up the fat globules so they are evenly distributed.

- Horeb (mountain): Desolate, drought, dry, heat utterly, waste. Scriptures, Exodus - Deuteronomy - 1 Kings - 2 Chronicles - Psalms - Malachi. Hebrew words:- (2717) - Chârâh; to parch (through drought), to desolate, destroy, kill:- decay, (be) desolate, destroy (-er), (be) dry (up), slay, surely, lay, lie, make waste. (2722)-Chôrêb; desolate, name for the Sinaitic mountains.

- Icons: Representation of Christ or a saint especially one painted in oil on a wooden panel - an image.

- Idol: Image, effigy or natural object worshipped as a god; heathen god; person or thing excessively adored or loved; widely excepted misconception or fallacy.

- Ideology:

Body of ideas forming basis for political, economic or social system; *(philosophy)* theory that all ideas derived from sensations; science of ideas; *(fig)* vague theorising, impractical views.

- Illuminati:

A group of persons claiming exceptional enlightenment on some subject e.g. religion.

- Inaugurated:

Duplicated, same as inauguration.

- Inauguration:

To commence officially - to place in office formally and ceremonially: induct, dedicate formally.

- Incantation:

Ritual recitation of magic words or sounds enchanting.

- Incumbents:

Occupying or holding an office especially a clergyman holding a benefice - to devote one's attention to.

- Indulgences:

R.C. Church, a remission of the temporal punishment for sin after guilt has been forgiven — A pleasure or habit.

- Ishmaelites:

A people who had Egyptian as well as Semitic blood in their veins. Characterised for their spirit of independence.

- Jesuits:

Member of R.C. religious order - defenders of Catholicism.

- Jewry:

Jews collectively - quarter of a town inhabited by Jews, Jewish religion or culture.

- Jezebel: Old Testament, The wife of Ahab, king of Israel — a shameless and scheming woman.

- Justification: Reasonable grounds for complaint, defence. Christian Theol., - the process of being justified or the condition of having been justified.

- Kingdom Now: Covers a wide variety of teachings. In general, it embraces a denial of the literal rapture, Antichrist, tribulation, thousand-year millennial reign of Jesus.

- Koran: The sacred book of Islam believed by Muslims to be the infallible word of god dictated to Mohammed.

- Literal Interpretation: Taking the plain meaning of the text, with consideration of the culture, background, and understanding of both the writer and the original recipient.

- Liturgy: The forms of public services officially prescribed by a church.

- Magnanimity: Generosity.

- Mediterranean: The sea between South Europe, North Africa and South West Asia — a native or inhabitant of *(Med)* Country a subdivision of the Caucasoid race.

- Messiah: The awaited King of the Jews, to be sent by God to free them - Hoped for liberator of a country or people.

- Middle East: Loosely - the area around the East Mediterranean - Israel, the Arab countries from Turkey to North Africa and Eastward towards Iran. Formally extending from Tigris - Euphrates to Burma.

- **Millennium:** A literal one thousand year period in which Jesus Christ will rule on earth after His literal return at the end of this age.

- **Mohammed:** The god of the Muslims.

- **Myrtle Tree:** An evergreen shrub of trees - a south European shrub with pink and white flowers and aromatic blue-blackberries.

- **Mythology:** A body of myths - study of myths.

- **Myths:** Story about superhuman beings of earlier age - a person or thing whose existence is fictional or unproven.

- **Nature of Antichrist:** Enemy of Christ or Christianity. One who is against Christ or a substitute for Him. Man of Sin, to defile the Temple.

- **Nazi:** A member of the fascist National Socialist German Worker's Party - under Adolf Hitler.

- **Nile:** A river, the second longest, flows 4,000 miles into the Mediterranean Sea.

- **Occult:** Same as Occultism.

- **Occultism:** Characteristic of mystical or supernatural phenomena of influences: secret or esoteric, to hide or become hidden or shut off from view.

- **Papacy:** The office or term of office of a Pope - a system of government in the R.C. Church that has the Pope as head.

- **Passover:** A festival instituted by God for Israel. An eight day Jewish festival, commemorating the sparing of the Israelites in Egypt *(death of the 1st born)*.

- Permutations: Do with maths.

- Persecution: To oppress, harass or maltreat - to bother persistently.

- Pharaoh: Someone who ruled over and even worshipped.

- Pharisees: Member of an ancient Jewish sect teaching strict observance of Jewish traditions.

- Phenomenon: Anything that can be perceived as an occurrence or fact by the senses - a thing as it appears, as distinguished from its real nature as a thing in itself.

- Philistines: A people who are hostile towards culture, the arts - people who are non-Semitic.

- Pilgrimages: A journey to a shrine or other sacred place - a journey or long search made for exalted or sentimental reasons.

- Placate: Appease the anger or resentment of. To pacify or appease.

- Placatory: From placates; trying to placate conciliatory.

- Post-Millennial: The Church will conquer and dominate the world, thus ushering in the visible Kingdom before the return of Christ. When the Church has fulfilled this task, then Jesus will return.

- Postulations: To assume, to be true or take for granted - to ask, demand or claim.

- Premillennial: The idea that Jesus returns before the thousand-year reign on earth. It is His coming that ushers in the visible aspect of the Kingdom.

- Presbyter: Elder in the Presbyterian or early Christian church; priest.

- Presbyterian: *(Member)* of a church governed by presbyters only.

- Priest: One whose office is to perform religious rites and offer sacrifice on behalf of the people; man empowered by ordination to consecrate the Eucharist and administer the sacraments; any Christian Cleric ranking above a deacon and below a bishop; ordain as priest, *(Alt., a fisherman's mallet).*

- Priesthood: Office of priest; order of priest; priests collectively.

- Principate: A state ruled by a prince - form of rule in early Roman Empire in which some republican survived.

- Profaned: Having or indicating, contempt, irreverence, or disrespect for divinity - coarse or blasphemous.

- Prophecy: A message of divine truth revealing God's Will - an act of uttering such a message - the charismatic endowment of a prophet.

- Proselytising: To convert one from one's faith to another.

- Purgatory: Chiefly R.C. Church - a state or place where the souls of those who have died in a state of grace are believed to undergo limited suffering or torment.

- Ramadan: A period of 30 days in the 9th month of the Muslim year, during which strict fasting is observed from Sunset to Sunrise.

- Rapture: Prior to the millennium Christ will remove the believing Church from the earth. Some place this event before the seven years of trouble, some during, some after.

- Reconstruction: Similar to Dominionism.

- Redeemed: Free from sin and death - Freed humanity.

- Redemption: The act or process of redeeming - deliverance from sin through the sufferings and death of Jesus Christ.

- Reformation: A religious and political movement of 16th Century Europe, began an attempt to Reform the R.C. Church and resulted in the establishment of the Protestant churches.

- Repudiation: 1) to reject the authority or validity of; refuse to accept or ratify 2) to refuse to acknowledge or pay a debt 3) to cast off or disown, a son, lover, etc.

- Restoration: A loose term, usually describing the ideas and efforts of some who align with the Kingdom Now faction.

- Reticent: Not communicative, not saying all that one knows - reserved.

- Revival: Act of reviving; state of being revived; return of life, vigour, popularity etc. New presentation, production etc; intensive campaign of sermons and prayer - meetings to rouse new religious fervour in a district.

- Revive: Return to life, health, consciousness, activity: flourish again; recover from neglect, depression, obscurity; re-awaken; bring back to life, popularity, activity; rouse; renew; produce again; restore to its natural *(or metallic)* state.

- Revivalist: One who organises meetings or preaches in a religious revival - revivalist.

- Saints: A person who after death is formally recognised by a Christian church as having attained a specially exalted place in heaven.

- Satanism: The worship, which includes blasphemous parodies of Christian prayers.

- Sinai: Hebrew *(5514)* - Cîynay - Sinai, a mountain of Arabia.

- Six, six, six (666): The mark of the beast.

- Socialism: An economic theory or system in which the means of production, distribution, and exchange are owned through the state.

- Stratification: To form or be formed in layers - divided into groups or to develop groups.

- Substantiate: Demonstrate the truth of, prove; make real.

- Substantiation: Proof.

- Substantive: Existing as a real and distinct being; expressing existence; naming a specific entity.

- Subterranean: Living or operating below the surface of the earth - concealment.

- Succour: 1) help or assistance especially in time of difficulty 2) a person or thing that provides help 3) to give aid to.

- Superstitions: Irrational belief usually founded on ignorance or fear.

- Superstitious: Disposed to believe a superstition.

- Symbolism: The bible does contain symbols. Occasionally the context demands symbolism *(example)*: "Learn the parable of the fig tree" *(Matthew 24:32).*

- Tabernacle: Old Testament portable sanctuary in which the ancient Israelites carried the Ark of the Covenant - Place of Worship - The Jewish Temple.

- Theocracy: Government by a deity or priesthood - a community under such government.

- Theonomy: The Law of God, especially as the Dominionists and Reconstructionists plan to re-establish Old Testament law over the nations, with themselves as the governors and judges administering these laws.

- Torah: The Pentateuch; the scroll on which it was written - The whole body of traditional Jewish teaching including the oral law.

- Transfiguration: New Testament. The change in the appearance of Christ that took place before three disciples *(Matthew 17:1-9).*

- Tribulation: Seven years of trouble on earth. Antichrist reigns. Pretribulationists believe the Church will be removed before the onset of the seven years.

- Unleavened Bread: Bread made from dough, which has no yeast.

- Vagabonds: A person with no fixed home, wandering beggar or thief.

- Vehemently:

  1) mark by intensity of feeling or conviction 2) of actions, gestures etc; characterised by great energy, vigour or force.

- Venerated:

  To hold in deep respect - to honour in recognition of qualities of holiness, excellence.

- Vicar of Christ:

  One of the titles that the Pope takes to himself, carries the meaning as "Antichrist" that is he who takes the place of or stands in for Christ.

- Yahweh:

  The next word for God is Jehovah or Yahweh, it speaks of His life and being. He is the being who is absolutely self-existent, the One who in Himself possesses essential life, permanent existence. He truly is the living God.

- Zion:

  The hill on which the city of Jerusalem stands - the ancient Israelites of the bible - the modern Jewish nation - the national home of the Jewish nation.

Endnotes

Preface

1. Appointment in Jerusalem, by Derek and Lydia Prince, Publisher: Chosen Books, Zondervan Publishing House, USA, 1975, p174

Chapter 1 Israel, the Church and the Endtimes

1. McAlvany Intelligence Advisor (October 1991), https://mcalvanyintelligenceadvisor.com

2. Taken from, Prince of Darkness, Antichrist and The New World Order, by Grant R. Jeffrey, ISBN: 0-921714-04-1, Publisher: Frontier Research Publications, Canada, 1994, p172

3. Prince of Darkness, Antichrist and The New World Order, p174

4. Sunday Express, by Oliver James, July 7th, 1996, p45

5. Prince of Darkness, Antichrist and The New World Order, p179-181

Chapter 2 Putin - Who is He?

1. Prophetic Vision. No.16 - Summer 2000, by David Hathaway, http://propheticvision.org.uk

Chapter 3 The War of Gog and Magog

1. Rushing to Armageddon, Prophecy 2000, by David Allen Lewis, ISBN: 0-89221-179-2, Publisher: New Leaf Press, USA, 1991, p37

2. Five Great Monarchies, by George Rawlinson, ISBN: 978-1402181412, Publisher: Adegi Graphics LLC, 1999, Assyria: Chapter 9, footnote

3. Hebrew and Chaldee Lexicon, by H. W. F. Gesenius, ISBN-13: 978-0801037368, Publisher: Baker Pub Group; 7th edition, 1990

4. Prince of Darkness, Antichrist and The New World Order, by Grant R. Jeffrey, ISBN: 0-921714-04-1, Publisher: Frontier Research Publications, Canada, 1994, p189

Chapter 4 The Rapture of the Church

1. Rushing to Armageddon, Prophecy 2000, by David Allen Lewis, ISBN: 0-89221-179-2, Publisher: New Leaf Press, USA, 1991, p244

Chapter 6 The Valley of Decision

1. Revelation: God's Grand Finale, by Hilton Sutton, ISBN: 0-89274-298-4, Publisher: Harrison House Inc., USA, 1984, p198

Chapter 7 The Millennium

1. The Thousand Years, by Nathaniel West, Publisher: Scripture Truth Book Company, 1950

2. Rushing to Armageddon, Prophecy 2000, by David Allen Lewis, ISBN: 0-89221-179-2, Publisher: New Leaf Press, USA, 1991, p256-257

3. The Meaning of the Millennium, by Herman Hoyt, ISBN-13: 978-0877847946, Publisher: IVP Academic; StIFF WRAPS edition, 1977

4. The Holy Spirit, by L. Thomas Holdcroft, Publisher: Gospel Pub House, 1979

5. Rushing to Armageddon, Prophecy 2000, p259

6. The Spirit Himself, by Ralph M. Riggs, Publisher: Gospel Publishing House, 1949, Chapter 25: The Holy Spirit in the Future, p190-191

7. Prince of Darkness, Antichrist and The New World Order, by Grant R. Jeffrey, ISBN: 0-921714-04-1, Publisher: Frontier Research Publications, Canada, 1994, p326

8. Prince of Darkness, Antichrist and The New World Order, p329

Chapter 8 Jerusalem, A Holy City

1. Revelation: God's Grand Finale, by Hilton Sutton, ISBN: 0-89274-298-4, Publisher: Harrison House Inc., USA, 1984, p220-222

Bible translations

- Unless otherwise indicated, all scriptural quotations are from the HOLY BIBLE, NEW INTERNATIONAL VERSION ®. NIV ®. Copyright © 1973, 1978, 1984 by the International Bible Society. Used by permission of Zondervan Publishing House. All rights reserved.

- Scripture references marked KJV are taken from the King James Version of the bible.

- Scripture references marked NKJV are taken from the New King James Version®. Copyright © 1982 by Thomas Nelson, Inc. Used by permission. All rights reserved.

- Strong, James. S.T.D., L.L.D. 1890. Strong's Exhaustive Concordance, Dictionaries (Lexicon) of the Hebrew and Greek Words.

Recommended Reading

- Ad Diem Illum Laetissimum, No14, by Pope Pius X
- Battle for Israel, by Lance Lambert
- Bless Israel for God's Sake, by Sven Nilsson
- Building a People of Power, by Ian Andrews
- Egyptian Religion, by Sir Wallis Budge
- Everyday Life in Babylonia and Assyria, by H.W.F. Saggs
- Fantasy Explosion, by Bob Maddux
- From Rock to Rock, by Eric Barger
- Growing in the Prophetic, by Mike Bickle with Michael Sullivant
- High-Lights of the Bible, by Ray C. Stedman
- Magnae Dei Matris, by Pope Leo XII
- Munificentissimus Deus, No20, by Pope Pius XII
- New Age to New Birth, by Roy and Rae Livesey
- Pagans and Christians, by Robin Lane Fox
- Prophecy Past and Present, by Clifford Hill
- Reflections on the Christ, by David Spangler
- Second Vatican Council, Dogmatic Constitution on the Church, No59

- Spiritual Mysteries Revealed!, by Morris Cerullo
- The Church of the Living God, by Ulf Ekman
- The God of Ecstasy, by Arthur Evans
- The Lion Handbook of the Bible
- The Mystery Religions, by S. Angus
- The New Cults, by Walter Martin
- The Plan and its Implementation, by M.E. Hazelhurst
- The Prophetic Ministry, by Ulf Ekman
- The Veneration of Mary; Our Lady of Perpetual Help; Our Lady of Perpetual Succor, by Pope Pius IX (compare these scriptures: Hebrews 7:25; Hebrews 13:5-6)
- The Women's Encyclopedia of Myths and Secrets, by Barbara Walker
- Toward a World Religion for the New Age, by Lola Davis
- Women's Dionysian Initiation, by Linda Fierz-David
- Wycliffe Bible Encyclopedia

Ministry Profile

Doctor Alan Pateman, an apostle, is the President and Founder of Alan Pateman Ministries International (APMI), which was established in England back in 1987, a Christian-based (parachurch) non-profit and non-denominational outreach. This ministry is now focusing in two main areas: Apostolic Networking (CFE) and secondly, the teaching arm, LICU University.

Connecting for Excellence International Apostolic Network is a multi-facetted missions organisation with the purpose of connecting leaders for divine opportunities and building lasting relationships, to touch the lives of leaders literally the world over. Apostle Alan has to date ordained more than 500 ministers in over 50 NATIONS. In addition there are ministries, churches and schools who are in Association or Affiliation, looking to him for apostolic counsel.

Secondly, **LifeStyle International Christian University,** which was founded in 2007, is a study program to help people discover their purpose and destiny. Doctor Alan holds the position of President/CEO, Professor of Theology, Biblical Studies and Apostolic Ministry. LICU is exploding throughout Europe, Asia and Africa, working with many churches.

He has authored more than 30 books including numerous teaching materials and university courses along with hundreds of Truth for the Journey articles on kingdom lifestyle *(that are regularly distributed globally via the internet).*

Doctor Alan is recognised as an Apostle, Bishop, Leadership Mentor, University Educator, Motivational Speaker, Connector and Author, who has also been featured on national and international TV and radio networks throughout the years.

Currently Apostle Alan, his wife Jennifer and three children reside in Florence, Italy and travel out from their Apostolic Company.

- Alan Pateman Ph.D., D.Min., D.D., M.A., B.Th.

To Contact the Author

Please email:

Alan Pateman Ministries International

Email: apostledr@alanpateman.com
Web: www.AlanPatemanMinistries.com

*Please include your prayer requests
and comments when you write.*

Other Books

Healing and Deliverance, A Present Reality

Within the pages of this book (which has to be a "must-read" for any serious enquirer into the Healing and Deliverance Ministry), Dr. Alan unfolds a different pathway, so that the heartbeat of God's message of God's total deliverance can be released into the church of Jesus Christ today.

ISBN: 978-1-909132-80-1, Pages: 188, Format: Paperback, First Print: 1994
Also available in eBook format!

Media, Spiritual Gateway

Let's face it; we live in the era of fake news! It's always existed, but never been quite so prominent. Today it's an all-out-war between fact and political fiction. The media has been sabotaged by political activism. Gone are the days of impartiality and objective unbiased reporting, with many sources saying that true journalism is dead.

ISBN: 978-1-909132-54-2, Pages: 192, Format: Paperback, Published: 2018
Also available in eBook format!

Truth for the Journey Books

Millennial Myopia, From a Biblical Perspective

The standard for every generation is Jesus. However Millennial Myopia describes the trap of focusing everything on one particular generation or demographic cohort, at the exclusion and expense of all others. The Church cannot afford to make this mistake too. Loaded with research, this book takes readers on a journey of discovery, revealing the true nature of kingdom diversity.

ISBN: 978-1-909132-67-2, Pages: 216, Format: Paperback, Published: 2017
Also available in eBook format!

The Age of Apostolic Apostleship Complete Series

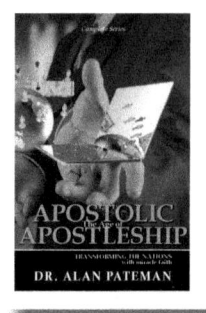

In order to view how the Apostolic baton was successfully passed from one generation to the next. Knowing that through the perseverance and obedience of others - history as we know it was altered forever. Dr. Alan Pateman, a modern day apostle (ascension) looks to reflect on their testimony in this wonderful book.

ISBN: 978-1-909132-65-8, Pages: 420
Format: Paperback, Published: 2017
Also available in eBook format!

TONGUES, Our Supernatural Prayer Language

In writing to the church at Corinth, Paul encouraged them to continue the practice of speaking with other tongues in their worship of God and in their prayer lives as a means of spiritual edification. "He that speaketh in an unknown tongue edifies, charges, builds himself up like a battery."

ISBN: 978-1-909132-44-3, Pages: 144, Format: Paperback, Published: 2016
Also available in eBook format!

LIFESTYLE UNIVERSITY | Raising Up Christian Leaders

Dear Friends,

Have you considered becoming one of our international students? We are privileged to welcome you, from around the world, to "LifeStyle International Christian University" *(the teaching arm of Alan Pateman Ministries International).* **An English speaking university** dedicated to your success; to see you trained and equipped to fully succeed in your God given Destiny.

It is our passion to raise up the leaders of tomorrow, who will have influence in all realms of authority, including the Body of Christ. Men and women of strategy, wisdom and true godliness, who'll stand with stature and maturity in this hour.

It's undeniable that in today's world, recognised education has become indispensable, therefore it is our desire to offer well balanced and well structured courses. Those that have been written by gifted and talented ministers of God, who seek to be inspired by God's Holy Spirit.

Consequently we have put together a **flexible curriculum,** designed both for correspondence students and extension campuses, which is a strategy to reach the distant learner; whether provincial, national or international. In fact we have many correspondence students from around the world, including a growing number of successful extension campuses, in various countries.

This is a growing platform, where men and women of dignity and passion, can grow and be established in their God given endeavours. As God is the healer of the nations, we pray and believe that many of our alumni will go on to **become world changers** in their own right.

We are proud of each and every one of our LICU students.
It would be our pleasure if you would join them on this incredible journey!

Doctor Alan Pateman

Alan Pateman Prof. Ph.D., D.Min., D.D., M.A., B.Th.
PRESIDENT AND CEO
www.licuuniversity.com www.cfeapostolicnetwork.com
Email: info@licuuniversity.com   Mob: +39 366 329 1315

For more information visit our website/facebook or contact our office, using the details below:

Website: www.licuuniversity.com
Facebook: www.facebook.com/LICUMainCampus
Email: info@licuuniversity.com
Telephone: +39 366 329 1315

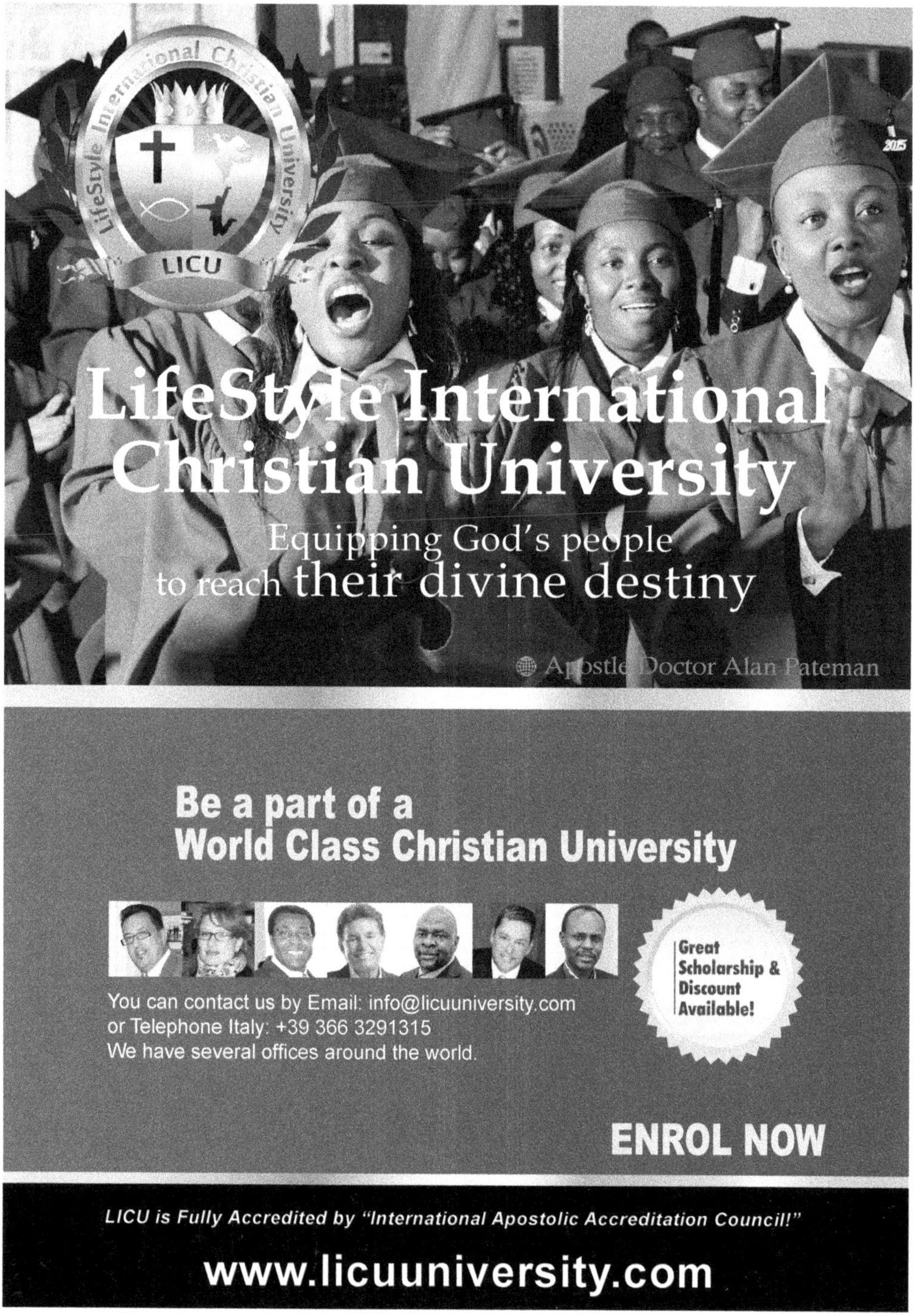

LifeStyle International Christian University

Equipping God's people
to reach their divine destiny

Apostle Doctor Alan Pateman

Partner with us TODAY!

We are looking to impact the world with the gospel, together we can do more! Join with us to equip the Body of Christ through our Apostolic Network, LICU university program, campuses, associated schools, missions, conferences, television programs, publication of articles and Truth for the Journey books.

You can become an APMI FOUNDATION PARTNER with a regular contribution of any amount, whether it is once a month or once a year.

- Receive monthly newsletters
- Connect with partners and leaders at our Connecting for Excellence international meetings
- Partners Dinners
- Personal availability for mentoring by Doctor Alan
- Enjoy complimentary books by Doctors Alan and Jennifer
- For those who GIVE EVERY MONTH £10, £15, £20, £30 or more will save money with special discounts on products, hotel rooms, conferences, and more

Partner With Us Today!
Call Italy: +39 366 3291315
Email: partners@alanpatemanministries.com
www.AlanPatemanMinistries.com

Bank Details:
Name: Alan Pateman
Bank Name: Deutsche Bank S.p.A.
IBAN: IT55F0310413700000000822953
BIC/SWIFT: DEUTITM1430

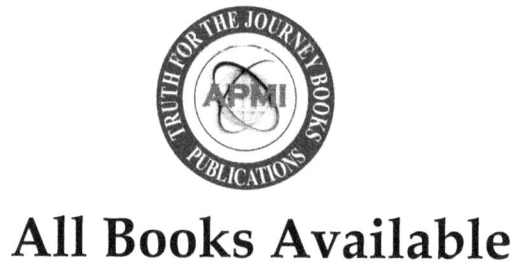

All Books Available

at

APMI PUBLICATIONS

Email: publications@alanpateman.com
Also Available from Amazon.com
and other retail outlets.

If you purchased this book through Amazon.com
or other and enjoyed reading it, or perhaps one of
my other books, I would be grateful if you could
take a couple of minutes to write a Customer
Review, many thanks.

www.ingramcontent.com/pod-product-compliance
Lightning Source LLC
Chambersburg PA
CBHW071559040426
42452CB00008B/1229